Published by Semiotext(e)
PO BOX 629, South Pasadena, CA 91031
www.semiotexte.com

Special thanks to Scott Cameron Weaver.

Cover Art: Calla Henkel & Max Pitegoff, 11 *Unused Glass Ashtrays*, 2022. Silver gelatin print, 26 1/2 x 22 1/2 x 1 1/3 in. Courtesy the artists and Galerie Isabella Bortolozzi, Berlin. Photo: Graysc / Dotgain.

Design: Hedi El Kholti

ISBN: 978-1-63590-190-0

Distributed by the MIT Press, Cambridge, Mass. and London, England
Printed in the United States of America

Artless

Stories 2019–2023

Natasha Stagg

semiotext(e)

Contents

Foreword

In Marguerite Duras's introduction to *Practicalities*, she writes (as translated from the French by Barbara Bray), "At most the book represents what I think sometimes, some days, about some things. So it does incidentally represent what I think. But I don't drag the millstone of totalitarian, i.e., inflexible, thought around with me. That's one plague I've managed to avoid."

Artless is a word often used to describe prose, as in ungainly, naïve, imprecise. This book is essentially a follow up to *Sleeveless: Fashion, Image, Media, New York 2011–2019*, a collection that, like this one, pieced together some inklings from the previous few years. It centers, necessarily, around a person and a period—me, now: a time when carelessness seems increasingly inexcusable. It elaborates on and possibly contradicts what I've written before. I considered calling it *Name Dropping* (one of my favorite pastimes, you'll see), but I couldn't resist generating some symmetry, as if I were naming pets. It is not without art, if I may say as much; it is, at times, uncareful, something I aspire to more frequently be.

I call these pieces "stories" because that's what they all are, even if they are musings, or reviews, or diaries. Some are more traditional short stories, completely made up, others real events superimposed with loose-fitting plots and characters based on no one or several people, and some are "what I think sometimes, some days, about some things." Nota bene: It doesn't matter what I think. Mostly, I think that I know nothing, and anyway, I will change my mind. My opinions should be fished out of this book and then thrown back. They are not, in my own estimation, of any importance.

What I've been thinking about, anyway, is work and what that has become, for everyone. What it was like, when it was easier, to separate jobs from opportunity, opportunity from experience. I'm thinking about writing as work and as entertainment and as a tool or a calling card. I write a lot of emails. I bet I have written hundreds of millions of emails. I would rather write books, but those are far less in demand. The pandemic was a lot of things, and that included a further enmeshing of such concepts, the eradication of compartmenting what one does and what one *does*. I wonder what work is, now, and I must admit that I don't want to know the extent of things. I've retreated a little. Regressed, maybe? If you do what you love, you'll never work a day, they say, or: if you never work a day, you're still doing something that might be considered work.

Last year, I was in a large studio outside of Paris. A model was being readied for an interview that would become behind-the-scenes clips for an advertisement. The brand team and I had gone back and forth in calls and shared documents about the questions that would eventually be asked on set. They needed to convey the essence of the product, using keywords, obviously. It, like her, was a next phase, a new icon, a timeless original.

I was dropped off by a hired driver and introduced to everyone. There was a small refrigerator of slim Coke cans and a spread of pastries, cold vegetables, and dips. I quickly realized, even if no one else had yet, that my presence was unnecessary, confusing even. A makeup artist trailed the model as she walked, touching up her blank expression with a fat brush. I had hoped for a smile suggesting recognition. Instead, she appeared tired and, as things progressed, uneasy. We were seated in canvas folding chairs facing one another about fifteen feet apart, so the cameras could capture her angles without me in them. I had to yell so she could hear me; she was pinned with a lavalier and could speak as quietly as she liked. The green screen behind her would end up some animation, which was yet unclear.

Who was I, she must have wondered, and why was I nervously asking her such strange, manufactured questions about the type of woman she was. Some corporate person would step in every time the model didn't want to respond, explaining why we'd come up with this avenue of discussion. I sat there, shrugging and smiling, holding a printout. Someone asked if she wanted the teleprompter. In the end, she reasoned, if we wanted her to say something about the thing we were selling, she would just say it. That's what she was getting paid for. And she did say it, first in a sultry voice, and then a serious voice, then an excited voice, then a bored voice, then in a babyish whisper. I was done and told I could wait outside for the car if I wanted. It was a sunny day, and a logo-patterned park bench from some other commercial was out there.

The model went back to work, twisting on a trapeze or whatever, while I looked at my dumb, overly edited questions, to which I didn't even want answers. The drive back to my hotel was long and relaxing. I thought about how maybe nothing was salvageable from this session. Likely, in fact, my entire trip had been ineffective. That we had failed to produce any bonus content and wasted so much time was terrifying, and so it was also exhilarating. We'd inadvertently proved some other point, perhaps.

Or, even better, we hadn't proved anything and the time that it took to achieve nothing had cost a relative fortune. I'm thinking about this scenario now because it was so padded with potentiality, so exemplary of a particular feeling the boundaries of which I'm trying to establish; capital is flowing in all directions, changing shape and shaping us, like a more physical kind of weather. The model, I'm sure, is used to this. Real, usable matter, she knows, is rare. Yet here I am remembering this fruitless day, buffing the memory with a fine grain to smooth its surface, fitting it, a little if not altogether artlessly, into an introduction.

Part 1

"I want to know why you are in a picture with Sarah Jessica Parker," my half-sister Roxy commented on my profile.

Two hours later: "This is my sister and she's fabulous."

I didn't respond to either comment, and one day was telling my boyfriend about how guilty I felt about that, but it was too late to do anything about it now, right?

"Tell me about this sister," he said.

"Half. She's older than me by about twenty years." I went through the bullet points that made everyone smile: She used to be a stripper, which is how she met her wife, the DJ at the club. She has breast implants and has talked about getting stars tattooed where her nipples are supposed to be, because she still doesn't have any. From there, it always gets dark: She keeps having to go back for more reconstructive surgery because of infection. She has a failing liver but hides liquor-filled water bottles in her car. Her son is married to a woman her age. Roxy and her daughter-in-law do not get along.

"I can't believe she's never come up," said my boyfriend. "Her real name is Roxy?"

"I shouldn't have said any of that. It's not like she's a freak, she's just a drunk."

"Is she still married?"

"Yeah. They're a good match." That night, I dreamt that I pulled up to my childhood home and found three dead bodies in a pool of blood so thick it was like a quicksand pit. My brother Mark cradled one of the bodies, the white one. "There's been a terrible car accident," he said.

"Where are the cars?" I asked. Roxy came out from the side of the house and looked longingly at the dead men. Everyone was talking and only one person was crying, but I couldn't tell who. My other brother, the oldest one, was alive in this dream. I tried to make myself cry.

"Who are they?" I asked.

Roxy started to sing a well-known song from the '80s, and her voice was as beautiful as the original version's. At the end she said, in her regular rasp, "That song was written about my friend."

"Do you remember when Roxy was on *Letterman*?" asked Mark.

Roxy looked wistfully away.

"No," I said.

A sped-up video of a young Roxy wearing a skin-tight dress that scooped low in the back played in my mind, as if Mark was playing it for me there. She spun in circles all over the stage.

I woke up and didn't tell my boyfriend about the dream because it was not about him or about sex. I went to work, where I had to sit with a team and try to come up with the headline for a magazine story about sisters.

"It sounds bad. Almost Jewish," said our boss.

"Their name is Arab, I think."

"What about something more obvious, like their first names? Let's make sure everyone just knows them by their first names," he interrupted.

"What is wrong with Jewish?"

"No one is listening to me," said our boss. "Let's use their first names."

"Not a problem," said my coworker. I was needlessly taking notes. "Just their names?"

"Yes," our boss sipped from a metal straw in a painted ceramic cup. He shook his head and then looked up. "I said yes."

"Michelle and Angela."

"The *elle-and-Ange* is a little—"

"I love it," said our boss. "Is anyone listening to me? I love it."

I left the meeting and went back to my desk, where I looked at a bunch of open tabs and refreshed them. "Please comment your celebrity stories," my friend's post said, for the sake of some art project she was working on. Most were about someone turning out to be short or a total bitch. A few, the more boring stories, sounded honest. Each story, by its very nature, sounded hopeful that the celebrity had been affected by the interaction.

Someone saw someone eating an ice cream cone on a bench in Park Slope. Someone returned someone's lost ID; he was a dick. Someone stared so hard at someone at an airport gate that he made her get up and sit somewhere else. Someone touched someone at his concert, and his hands were smaller than hers. Someone asked someone for a ride to set and she told him no. Someone tried to steal someone's suitcase at O'Hare. Someone was like five people in front of someone in line for a roller coaster and he shut the ride down so he could ride alone with his girlfriend. Someone sold someone a very expensive dress and she paid for it in cash. Someone saw someone at a party and asked her about the elevator story and she said, "I'll tell you this: he deserved it." When someone was on a game show, he told the host he liked his tie and the host said, "Yes. It looks like planets."

For my contribution, I wrote about the time I met Sarah Jessica Parker. It was at a fashion show's after-party, but the guests were mostly not A-list or even any list, just New York nightlifers and press. I went with a friend, who was invited by the designer.

I went outside to smoke a cigarette by myself. It was quiet and pretty. I could make out boats drifting along the river by their lights. My friend came out to find me. I started to tell him something, then interrupted myself to say, "I think that's Catherine Keener," about a woman standing a few feet away in cargo pants and Tevas.

"Who's Catherine Keener?" he asked.

"Haven't you seen *Walking and Talking*?"

"No."

Catherine Keener noticed me talking about her and walked up to us and said, "Hi, I'm Catherine. Catherine Keener."

I said, "I know, I'm a fan."

"No, you didn't know who I was," she argued.

"Yeah, you're really famous, and I was just telling him two seconds ago that you're one of my favorite actors," I said.

"I'm not famous," she said. I wanted to say that she's won an Oscar, but I wasn't sure if that was true, so I didn't.

"What is this, anyway? Some kind of a party?"

"It's for a fashion show," I said.

"Oh, that makes sense, you're models," said Catherine.

I laughed and looked at my friend, who looked away.

"I'm just here to meet my friend Sean, Sean Avery," she said. "He lives upstairs."

"The hockey player?" I said, but she didn't hear me. Sarah Jessica Parker had walked out and cameras were flashing, so Catherine turned to look.

"Oh, that's my friend Sarah, I didn't know she was here," said Catherine. "You have to meet Sarah. She's not going to turn and look this way, though, until her bodyguard tells the paparazzi that they have to stop. She told me this before: You can't look away, or they'll catch you making a face that looks upset, or, you know, ungrateful."

A man emerged from behind Sarah and held his hand up.

The flashes ceased. Sarah stepped lightly down the steps in a daze, but soon recognized Catherine.

"Cathy!"

"Sarah!"

They embraced. Sarah looked even tinier in Catherine's arms. "I want you to meet my friends." Catherine said our names to Sarah.

"Oh, that's right," said Sarah. "I've heard about you."

"I just met them," said Catherine.

"No, no," said Sarah, rolling her eyes. "Isn't this … ?"

"I swear to god, I just met them," Catherine argued.

They talked for a few minutes about their children and school schedules, and then seemed to realize that it might be wiser to go upstairs, where the hockey player Sean Avery lived. During that window of time, though, a photographer from the *New York Times* took a picture, and in it, the four of us look like friends.

On my friend's post, I wrote that I met Sarah Jessica Parker through Catherine Keener, and that she is even smaller than you think.

My Best Friend in High School

Candy had a CD in her hand when she got in my car, the car I always borrowed when I was home for the holidays. We were in the parking lot of a pizza place after her first day working there. As I drove, she skipped the songs faster and faster, until she couldn't have heard even the first phrase of any of them. "This CD sucks, I forgot." I tried to think of anecdotes from the evening before, from my own family's Thanksgiving dinner. All of it sounded so boring in my head, though. Even that we ate Thanksgiving dinner on the day the rest of the world did sounded boring.

Home was always paler than I remembered it to be when I came back from college for the breaks. Candy always brought me to her family's Thanksgiving, which was at a Japanese restaurant. The family consisted of Candy's older sister Cassie, their half-brother Timothy, and their mother Sheryl, who always brought someone, or rather, she had someone bring her. This year, it was Pete, who was a large man, with inflated jowls and a deep laugh. He seemed to be well liked, which probably meant he had money.

I parked crookedly and Candy said I should re-park, but when I started to back up, she said not to bother. We walked toward the restaurant, a short, wide building with orange koi painted on the black wooden doors. She was quiet as we walked, but she took my hand, and I squeezed it. I asked how work was and she said, "Stupid." I asked if she'd really worn sweats to her first day and she said, "Why not?"

Sheryl almost didn't remember my name, even though I'd known her since I was fourteen. When the waiter arrived, I realized that the restaurant was empty except for the people at the bar and us.

"I'll have a white wine," I said.

"You're old enough to drink already?" asked Sheryl.

"I'm a few months older than Candy," I answered.

Sheryl laughed, "Candy can drink." Whenever she spoke, she dragged out the last sound of each sentence, which annoyed her children and charmed me. A lot of things about her were like that, like how she was always tan and only wore white. The first time I'd been invited to her house, Sheryl offered me a Xanax.

Cassie asked how school was going and if I had a boyfriend.

"Well, and no. I just broke up with someone."

"Oh, good, right? Fuck boys, and all that shit?" Cassie was the more popular sister. It was a rivalry that hardly existed because of its imbalance.

When we graduated from high school, I started college and Candy started cocaine. She overdosed, and her father treated it the same way he'd treated her suicide attempts, by sending her to a mental institution. She was released after three months, around the time I was coming home from my freshmen year of college for the summer. I picked her up in my aunt's car. I asked her what it was like, and her eyes wouldn't meet mine while she talked. The adult ward was much different from juvenile, she said. I guess she was telling me that she was scared straight, but she no longer looked scared to me.

Her dad's new house smelled like her. It surprised me that Candy could take that smell to another location, and that it could linger without her. This smell was my idea of femininity and youth: not vanilla-lavender-rose-lace Victoria's Secret sprays, and not kiwi-strawberry-coconut Lip Smackers in glittery plastic Caboodles. It was saltine crackers, acrylic paint, canned tomato soup, cigarettes, and a sour note, like the fluids we used in the school dark room. We put on old satin nightgowns and sat in front of Candy's little white TV. Her father wasn't home yet. "I have to tell you something," she said into a pillow. She laughed, and then stopped. "I thought about you all the time. When I went to sleep, I masturbated under the covers. I think the night staff liked that, those sick fucks. I only thought about us, though."

I was telling Cassie about the guy I'd dated the first half of my sophomore year of college. She asked if we broke up because he was mean.

"No, just kind of boring," I said.

"Pete's not bo-reeng," interjected Sheryl.

"No one said he was, Mom," said Candy.

"Look at these pictures I took of him," she giggled, and passed her cell phone around the table. "They're really cute. He looks like Bruce Springsteen."

"Mom," said Cassie. "Are these pictures of Pete naked?"

She was brushing her hair again and taking a pen out of her purse. Timothy passed the phone back to Pete without looking at it.

"Pete," said Cassie. "Did you want my mom to show us those?"

"He doesn't cay-er," said Sheryl. "Hey Anika, now that you're not dating anyone, you should date Timothy." This had happened before, which is why Timothy and I had never had a conversation. We each stared at our plates.

"I'm going to pee," suggested Candy. "Come with me." Once inside the handicapped stall, we talked about comparing our vaginas, since we hadn't in a while. I said I didn't want to shave mine any-more because it wasn't worth it if I didn't have a boyfriend, and she said she always shaved hers just in case. She showed me before she sat on the toilet and I said it looked like she'd never had any hair there. I only flashed mine before I sat down.

"I didn't even see it!"

"It looks gross right now."

"So?" A lady in the stall next to ours flushed. "Show me now."

"I'm peeing."

"Show me!" She pushed my torso back, so my pee streamed forward and hit the seat and part of my thighs. The lady was still washing her hands.

"I saw it," said Candy. She turned to leave, and I had to remind her that she had to wait until I was done because the door only locked from the inside. We walked back to the table, Candy in front of me. When we sat down, she told everyone there what had happened and that we didn't wash our hands, but no one was listening.

In high school, I knew I wanted to be with Candy. I'd been with boys but never really had a boyfriend and didn't think I would ever start wanting one. She was beautiful then. We decided that we would go on a real date after having been friends for almost two years. I drove to her dad's apartment complex in a tight black dress with mesh sleeves. I pictured her wearing the white cotton dress with eyelets and green rosettes around the neck she usually hung up on her closet door. I imagined that this was a special enough occasion to finally put it on. I was let in by Cassie, who wrinkled her brow when I asked where Candy was. "She's in our room," she sighed.

Framed prints from furniture stores, the watercolors of rivers near barns and tree-lined Parisian streets decorated the walls. I climbed past them, smelling my own citrusy perfume mix with the apartment's smells. I admired my own freshly painted nails as I grabbed the room's doorknob, flung it open. I found Candy there, naked, although I couldn't immediately discern this, seeing first a flexing, sweaty male body covered her. I heard a girlish moan and turned away, meaning to run out of the house. Before I could, though, I heard Candy's voice again. "Hey," she squealed, happily. "You're here!"

I spent the next hour sobbing into a pillow on her bed, waiting for Candy to say the right words as she pet my head. The boy lived just down the street and left without much need for an explanation from anyone. I think I might have been more in love with Candy then than I was ever in love with anyone. I could not be anywhere, even there, that she wouldn't have made better.

On the Greyhound heading back to school, I called my favorite college friend.

"How's the fam?" he asked.

"It's so nice to hear your voice," I exhaled dramatically.

"How's Candy?" Of course I'd told him about her.

"She's exactly the same," I said.

"Good. I don't want her to get all sane before I even meet her." Poor Josh. I was sure she would hate him. He met me at the station, and we carried my bags down the street to my house, crunching fresh snow that had turned everything bluish white or wet black. "So, is she going to visit anytime soon?" Candy had asked me several times if she could come see me, to check out the school, to meet my new friends. I'd always managed to find ways of coming to her first.

"You know, she's never left the state?"

"How is that possible?" Josh asked. "Her family never went on vacation?"

"No." Now I could never introduce them because he would bring that up to her.

"That's insane," he said, and I felt like he was talking about my own family, but I agreed, and started listing the places my family had taken me as a kid.

The Dollhouse

Speaking with a man who had been "cancelled," as he described it, I realized he wanted something from me. Validation, maybe, like another signature on the petition in his mind that says he's not the crazy one. I kind of know how that feels, but I don't know exactly how it feels. It's true that abuse of power should come as no surprise, and it is also true that with power comes a type of knowing. I do not know what it feels like to be a man, to be told you are privileged when you feel like nothing. I do not know what it is like to have my personal life shamed by my peers and colleagues. I guess I wouldn't wish it on anyone if I really thought about it. But at the same time, I want some men to suffer. I would like for the trauma-bonded coalition that has been forming since the start of the hashtag movement to stop their whining. They can at least stop talking to me about it. "I've been slighted, too," I said to this cancelled guy.

"Well, I'll tell you what," he responded, not in response. "If I had known that some women only go to those parties to further their careers, I wouldn't have gone to them myself."

I have a friend, a publicist, who broke up with a man who said #MeToo was a racist conspiracy to take down Black men, mostly. He had been converted by Kanye West to Trumpism, unaware of the term. He was vocally incensed over the Brett Kavanaugh hearing, saying women had victimized him more than the other way around, and that this was another example of women getting away with something hurtful in the name of feminism.

"Don't let me do that again," said the publicist, a smart person, about dating the ex.

"Isn't it easy not to?" I asked.

She gave me a look, which was to remind me that a few years ago, I had slept with this guy, too.

I was having dinner with a group of friends and acquaintances when the ousted publisher of an art magazine came up in conversation, and we all had to decide, privately, if we would still want to cancel him if his story were newly revealed now. "He was genuinely creepy," said a stylist.

"It was bad behavior, enough to get fired over," said a showroom director.

The stylist's boyfriend, a retoucher living in France, was confused.

"He was being manipulative to a lot of women," I tried to explain. "But more importantly, it was an early event on the timeline."

In France, the movement is slightly different in scope, and called, if translated to English, "Out Your Pig." Outing someone is generally considered violent, which maybe explains why so many French women, mostly movie stars and writers who had once been famous for their sex appeal, resisted this movement, calling it prohibitive to progress. A group of gorgeous Parisian luminaries signed a petition stating that Out Your Pig caused more harm than good. They called for protesting the protests, calling out call-out culture.

I sometimes write for French magazines and work for French brands, so I often get emails from France. One email asked if I would consider interviewing one of the petition signers about the anniversary of her memoir. Another email asked if I wanted to interview a French director who appeared to be courting cancellation.

Yet another email asked me to interview an American director who had loudly participated in the Time's Up campaign. I declined each request, unsure of what I wanted to ask or hear from these people.

"Enough is enough, right?" said the retoucher. His question was innocent. He had assumed we would all be protective of the men who didn't rape or blackmail but were shamed, nonetheless. The movement had started innocently, too, I said, as an actionable antidote to the authority figures that endlessly fail powerless girls. It was a revelation, then, I continued. All these women could talk freely about how weird it was that their boss was behaving a certain way, how weird it was that it seemed acceptable to become so personally involved in your employees' social lives. All these women had translated it to art-world-weird when really it felt, in its aftermath, infantilizing and rude, a violation.

Even while I spoke, though, I thought of the publisher at a fashion magazine for which I once worked. No one seemed to mind his suggestive jokes and the hilarious memes he shared about getting shitfaced and desperate. He even dated a young intern, I think.

"Okay but does this man have to be cancelled for life?"

"He was fired, but he's alive," someone offered.

"I've always anticipated that anyone could be fired for less," I said. "Office politics are all about smear campaigns."

The retoucher, a freelancer, was not convinced. "Smear campaigns shouldn't be okay, though." I know, I know, I wanted to say. It will be all right in the end. Nothing will really change.

My registered-libertarian ex-boyfriend once explained the Trump thing to me as the first time any of these lower-class white people got to feel like a part of a subculture, which is an intoxicating experience no one should be deprived of. "I remember when I first discovered punk," he said. "If I could relive that, I would."

"But punk is mostly lower-class white people," I said.

"Honestly, I'd rather work in the yard with some Trump guy from Queens than a Williamsburg hipster who just learned how to weld," he said.

"But you live in Williamsburg, and you started welding last year," I said.

"Exactly."

My coworker and I were sitting in a park in SoHo, eating lunch on our break. "Should I be offended that this guy asked me to get him onto the Shitty Media Men list?" she asked.

A group of high school kids were sitting on the other benches in the park, eating ice cream. A short, bearded man with a British accent was telling them to gather 'round. "Get the fuck over here," he said, "so I don't have to yell like an idiot." They complied, getting closer and closer until I couldn't hear anyone's voices.

"It's over now anyway," I said to my friend. "The Shitty Media Men List is cancelled. And we were never invited to see it."

"Well, this guy wants to be on it," said my coworker. "He thinks it would help his career."

"What does he do?"

"I think he's an art handler," she said, maybe forgetting what we were talking about.

I illegally lit a cigarette. "Maybe he should start a Shitty Women in Art list."

The bearded British man and the horde of children wearing soft tracksuits started to walk, as a group, out of the park, silently.

I have a friend, a housewife, who has lived all over suburban Middle America. She called me the other day and said that her neighbor, a man, beat her up while her husband was out of town for work. The children were at school.

"Everyone out here voted for Trump," she said, "and the thing is they voted for him because of the personal stuff. Of course all men say that pussy-grabbing kind of shit when they think no women are listening. I know that that wasn't his platform, and I shouldn't pay that much attention to it because it was said in private, and look at what I say in private, but these guys out here where I live, they do pay attention to it. They fucking love it. They started paying attention when they heard he'd said that shit and they were like, Hell yeah."

She'd gotten into an argument with her neighbor over the president. Since she lived next door, she knew all this guy's extramarital secrets, so when things got heated, she had threatened to reveal them to everyone. That's when he ran into her house through the backyard and choked her until she saw stars. She didn't call the police because she didn't want to start a bigger feud. When her husband came back from his work trip, he beat up the neighbor while she watched.

Months after our only date, I received a paragraph-long text from a self-described Tim Allen fan at three in the morning. It ended with a cloying, "I think we had a nice time, right?" I got the sense that he needed the proof for some reason.

Another text, from a different potential suitor, read, "I wanted you to know I think about you often." It sounded like it would be said through clenched teeth. This one was from a guy who, on our first of two dates, complained about how much of his money his ex-wife spent on their kid.

A guy I slept with twice didn't contact me again until he saw my book at the Strand. "Did you buy it?" I asked. He hadn't, but he wanted me to know that he did buy a book, and that it was by another female author, one who was dead.

I had wanted leverage, and in some cases I had it. But all the men around me had started to act like scared animals, whimpering and then snapping. When I was asked to write something about cancel culture, I recoiled. I don't want to say anything that isolates someone or hurts someone or dismisses someone, in theory. I say "in theory" because I know that it is impossible to create a universally inoffensive document.

I like the idea of creating all new sets of standards with which to align, exploding a system of binaries. This was the dream of the anonymous public call-out, which offers gradations to issues that demand a more complex response than a yes or no vote. I like the concept of participating in a conversation instead of running to a cop, offering one takedown at the risk of being taken down ourselves, by way of social media. That's an idealistic view of something that relies on a system of sensationalism and exists within an algorithm, though.

Dreams of eliminating chauvinism by essaying about it were eventually dashed by a chorus of catfights in an echoing alley: screams circling a chamber, or a void, as we all like to say now. The problem, though, is that nothing is void when you say it online. As a society, we have had to learn that the only way to dodge cancellation is with distraction. Saturate with scandal.

"Let me tell you about the way this Nabokov thing played out," a man I'd just met said.

"On Twitter?" I asked, and then, to make sure he knew my stance, "I love *Lolita*."

"It started with an essay." He then told me about the author of said essay, who was a woman he personally didn't like.

There was another thing happening that was supposed to align people against a Democratic presidential candidate because he'd said he loved *Ulysses*, which is apparently too highbrow for a politician. So now I've not only seen someone describe the Joyce novel as a long-winded telling of a white male cuck farting into a toilet, but I've seen many people agree that this was an adequate summary of its seven hundred pages.

As one writer put it, in a takedown piece about takedown threads, "a dramatically reductive view of the past is very much in keeping with a particular kind of anti-intellectualist sentiment—the one that assumes, or pretends to assume, that no one actually likes 'difficult' books or movies or art, and that they are only saying they do in order to seem smart or trick someone into having sex with them." People are naturally skeptical of things they do not understand, like books they have not read, or what it is like to have power.

Someone else was trying to convince me that a famous writer was shitty because their Twitter account sucked.

"Their books are brilliant," I said.

"I've never read one," he said.

"In high school, they meant so much to me."

"We can't always trust the opinions of people we used to love in high school," he countered.

"Reading a novel is not listening to a person's opinion," I said, my voice shaking.

He told me a story about a Ukrainian artist who did not understand why Martin Luther King Jr. wasn't cancelled posthumously after it was revealed that he had cheated on his wife. "It just goes to show you that context is everything," he said.

"I think that proves my point, actually," I said.

"I didn't know we were making points," he said.

On an old episode of *90 Day Fiancé: The Couples Tell All*, an American man who is thirty-nine years older than his teenage

Filipino bride says, "I know it must be hard for American women to understand this." As I watched, the smirk on his face sent me into a rage. The age of consent differs from country to country and state to state, which really tells us that our understanding of consent as a concept is fluid. Age is fluid too, and yet it is difficult to see outside of our own fixed ages.

As a young woman, I was involved in an affair. The most exciting part was that we would have to sneak around, in hotel rooms, on secret trips. It was difficult for me to empathize with the unsuspecting wife, who was older than both of us, and who surely at some point could never imagine herself as the age she was, in the situation she was in. *The other woman* is a category usually relegated to younger women, and I was ecstatic to be young. One day, I thought, I will be old, and then I will be cheated on. It was my justification for acting erratically back then, even if someone had to suffer for my indiscretions. I was easily seduced by an unattainable man with worldly connections.

When I got older, a man cheated on me with a few younger women. I had never really thought it could happen to me, it turns out, because the information shocked me. The man had easily seduced these younger women by evoking unattainability, world-liness, and connections.

My initial reaction was panic. My age had become the other one: old. My next response was anger. I wished I could have revenge without having to orchestrate it. If only this type of behavior was unauthorized. Coincidentally, immediately following the revelation of this affair, my ex's boss was fired for hitting on employees. He had to make a public apology. Maybe I could just wait and see what happened. The next thing that happened was that my ex quit his job to become a ghostwriter and stopped all his social media accounts. I never heard from him again.

Now that I have some distance, I can see that if I had made an effort to shame this person, I would have been a hypocrite in some ways. Not to say that my actions at one age are what must determine my convictions at another. What I mean is that a power imbalance is one of the most commonplace aphrodisiacs. Far be it from me to deprive anyone of a little fun, even at the expense of others, even at the expense of me.

Another story: A few years ago, a man I thought I was in love with dumped me. I was taken off guard when he told me, mid-coitus in his Bel Air basement, that it wasn't going to work out between the two of us. He said it matter-of-factly, though, as if I was obviously going to agree, maybe ecstatically—like a verbal confirmation of our shared detachment would intensify our intercourse.

He was surprised when I started to get upset, and maybe more surprised when I didn't want him to stop fucking me. It was the night before he was to drive me to the airport so I could fly back home. I couldn't sleep, though, and didn't want to talk to him after that, so I asked if I could watch a movie on his laptop while he dozed off next to me.

I wanted to feel like at least I had New York, like I was going back to something wonderful, so I watched *Manhattan*. Nearing the end, I silently cried because I was in bed with a man who didn't love me but also because I loved New York—the city, and the way it is depicted in movies, and the memories of the first time I saw each.

I loved Woody Allen for making this thing for me to return to. At the same time, I could imagine that it would be painful to watch this if I was someone else: someone related to or married to or an ex of Woody's, for example, or if I was someone who was manipulated by an older man or left for a much younger woman and felt stunted by either experience. I could understand why every movie could be a bad time for someone.

I could even understand why people who had no citable experiences pertaining to this narrative felt oppressed by the cult of Woody Allen and his legacy. Anything so influential becomes an artifact consisting of its elements and their historical aftereffects. Everything overexposed is eventually stale.

Watching *Manhattan* at that time put me in reverie, though. Even then, I vaguely knew that the man sleeping next to me would always be another thing to return to in future moments of despair, a memory of a meaningful time.

I would later realize that what I had mistaken for love was actually an emotional attachment to an earlier experience with another movie, anyway—one in which this guy was an actor. I had been dating the grown-up version of my childhood crush. What I mean is that he costarred, as a fourteen-year-old, in a movie I first watched when I was fourteen years old, and I'd been in love with him ever since.

In *Welcome to the Dollhouse*, the bully character tells the dork character that he's going to rape her after school. She shows up, afraid but also eager for a diversion from her miserably typical suburban childhood. She tries to impress the bully, who is appalled by her lack of awareness, but touched, too, by someone displaying eager interest in him. I identified with the nerd at that age, having been thrown into a trite suburban landscape and desperate for a violent awakening. Later, I moved out of the suburbs. My first year in New York, I met Brendan, the actor who played the bully. By Christmas, I was staying with him in LA.

I closed the laptop and tried to sleep. The sun curled down the valley and bounced off the pool outside, sparkling ostentatiously until Brendan finally woke up. We drove through Bel Air's green hills and painted gates, the entrance flanked by faux Spanish monuments, pillars to a type of design that meant something else a long time ago. We stopped so I could buy three packs of cigarettes because they were cheaper in California.

I realized, after months of feeling devastated by the breakup, that my crush was always on the bully character Brendan played, not Brendan himself. I still can't really tell the difference sometimes. Even his Staten Island accent was put on, an exaggerated version of the one he'd had to neutralize when he started acting as a teen.

Anyway, during our short relationship, my fantasy was played out in full. I was the uncool nobody, harboring feelings for an early representation of deviance in my coming-of-age: the classic tough exterior that gives way to a fragile ego. He was out of my league, but worried about being washed up, and captivated by my infatuation. I was ecstatic to be on a date with a facsimile of my dream guy and he was entertained by how nervous I was on our dates, reliving a type of stardom. We took advantage of one other. Although the dynamic was exciting to me and to him for very different reasons, all those reasons were on the table from the start. There were times when the way he treated me didn't seem fair and I was upset by the imbalance. There were other times when I wished he were treating me unfairly, since that more closely resembled the character that I was initially attracted to.

Brendan didn't love it when people asked him to say his pivotal line from *Welcome to the Dollhouse*, and understandably. Ever since he had uttered, at fourteen, "I'm gonna rape you, three o'clock, be there," he'd been typecast as a psychopath, even though his character's ignorant use of the word "rape" was part of a portrait of lower-class insecurity. The bully is a hopeless, outcast kid who resorts to empty threats and naïve propositions under stress. The line has had to age into an atmosphere where wordings are more closely watched. Perhaps, in this context, the story of an adolescent performance of masculinity meeting a misguided rape fantasy isn't as heart-warming as it used to be, but it will always resonate with me since I am a product of my experiences. I will always have the movie, the memory of the first time I saw the movie, a casual friendship with the lead male actor from the movie, and the memory of the first time he whispered in my ear, "I'm gonna rape you, three o'clock, be there." I wouldn't change any of it.

Difficult

"Who cares about your stupid problems? You have to make people care about your stupid problems," says Elizabeth Wurtzel, sitting across from me at Claudette. The waitstaff there knows her by name and doesn't mind that she brings her large dog Alistair inside with her. At fifty-one, Elizabeth is as blonde as ever, with pretty, wide-set eyes that inspired a casting director to find Christina Ricci for the 2001 movie version of her young life. That film ("I thought it was really bad, a really dumb movie, and nothing like the book," she says of it now) was based on her first memoir, *Prozac Nation*, which turns twenty-five this year, the age Elizabeth was when she finished writing it. At twenty-six, she was catapulted into fame both literary and sexy, a Harvard graduate and *Rolling Stone* journalist who'd published the document that 1994 was dying for: a true account of growing up depressed, dissatisfied, and medicated.

Everyone cared about her so-called stupid problems then, and because of her role in co-narrating the Gen X experience, many still do. Her latest essay, published by *The Cut* in late 2018, is a juicy account of Elizabeth's discovery that her biological father was actually the activist photographer Bob Adelman, not Donald Wurtzel, the man she (and he) grew up thinking of as her dad. In this piece, her mother divorced Donald when Elizabeth was two, racked by guilt over the affair she'd had with Bob, which conceived their daughter. This was kept a secret from Donald and from anyone who would have let on that their broken marriage—a major topic in *Prozac Nation*—was unfixable for such a tangible reason.

The life described in *Prozac Nation* was painful, at times inexplicably so. But that Donald Wurtzel went to his grave thinking Elizabeth, the prolific writer of real-life family drama, was his daughter, and that Bob Adelman, the prolific civil rights documentarian, went to his grave knowing that she was really his, adds some weight to the narrative. No one else in Elizabeth's life could figure out why she was so unhappy in her skin—and here, perhaps, was some semblance of an answer. But for Elizabeth, it's not that easy. Nothing ever is. "I aced the wrong problem," she says, when I ask how this revelation has affected the way she now sees her memoirs. "But that's kind of not true, because he was my father. I mean, he is my father. My father who isn't really my father? He's my father." And then: "I still haven't heard from my stepmother. I think she probably saw [the essay]. She was always wretched to me."

Elizabeth's raw vulnerability (in her writing and in person) links her to today's authored identity, the aftermath of a cultural shift toward accepting our modern state of constant surveillance. If privacy is already dead, the idea of writing a tell-all is logically easier to stomach. Self-publishing realistic portrayals of one's own life, in real time, is now to be expected from writers and nonwriters alike. As a precursor to all this, though, *Prozac Nation* birthed countless authors now notorious for exposing the uncomfortable details of their privileged upbringings and subsequent adjustment issues. "I think Cat Marnell is very gifted and I think she needs to work," says Elizabeth as an aside, and: "I don't think of Lena Dunham as a writer on the page, but she's amazing on the screen."

It's easy to compare Elizabeth to young writers now, but in the '90s, she tells me, no one compared her to whom she should have been compared to, seeing as she didn't write fiction and wasn't a man. "Whether it's Dave Wallace or Rob Bingham or John Franzen or Rick Moody, they all are people who do the same kind of work I do. People think what they do is better, but I think that's nonsense. I don't think what they do is better. I don't even think that what they do is so much different. But if people think it's better, I think that's bullshit. They're sexist."

She's been called difficult, she says, all her life. "The most difficult thing about me is my reputation for being difficult. I don't think I'm that difficult. I don't know any women who aren't complained about as being difficult, whoever they are. That's it. That's the word on any woman who has any kind of reputation. It's so boring. Possibly all women who are successful are difficult. Maybe all men who are successful are difficult. It might be that all people are difficult."

For more on this, see her second book, *Bitch: In Praise of Difficult Women*, which sorts out her feelings on characters as disparate as Hillary Clinton, Amy Fisher, and Nicole Brown Simpson. The 1999 paperback is prefaced with press clips, categorized as "the Good," "the Bad," "the Bitchy," and "the Bottom Line". (An example of the Good: "The Courtney Love of letters." An example of the Bad: "in serious contention to usurp Camille Paglia as the loud-mouthed loose cannon of pseudointellectual quasi-feminist cultural criticism.") Back then, Elizabeth was compared to the long-dead Sylvia Plath ("… with the ego of Madonna") and the songwriter Bob Dylan, not her literary contemporaries. "Well, Dylan did win the Nobel Prize for Literature in 2016," I have to interject, which gets her onto the topic of Joan Didion. "When I say, 'Why is nobody upset that Didion hasn't gotten a Nobel?' people are like, 'Well, she has to write fiction.' First of all, she does write fiction. Second of all, does Bob Dylan write fiction?"

Prozac Nation is a time capsule. Today, we're well versed in the terminology surrounding social anxiety, body dysmorphia, and chemical imbalances, but in the '90s, before prescription advertisements, the term *attention deficit disorder* was just a twinkle in the eye of many a hyperactive child and Prozac was being hocked, hardly a question asked, to teenaged girls with distant stares in psychiatrists' offices. Adults were ever more isolated from their Walkman-wearing kids by having to recognize a host of new learning disabilities. Because of the way the industry was taking shape, physicians couldn't resist incentivized drug programs, and a generation was being defined by its diagnoses before its symptoms. Elizabeth was a teenager in the '80s and depressed before that, growing up on the Upper West Side and writing for a few notable magazines as a student. In the '90s, she declared herself a star pupil of the school of pills and rock music, and as a young twenty-something, she was everywhere—beautiful, young, invited—while publicly suffering from addiction and by all accounts an inflated ego. Her story was somehow proffered as both a commendable career and a cautionary tale.

The day before we met up, Elizabeth let me know that her life was overwhelming at the moment. Since the *Cut* piece, her relationship with her mother had been strained. She was still undergoing breast cancer treatment after a double mastectomy. Her husband of three years had recently moved out of their apartment. Seeing that apartment, I couldn't imagine anyone else living there. Just about every inch of every wall was covered in framed images of Elizabeth herself, from early press pictures to book cover outtakes to wedding photos. A cat and Alistair chased each other around couches covered in butterfly-embroidered cushions. A few cocktails into our meeting, she deadpanned, "I'm not impressed by the fact that my husband thinks I'm *difficult*. I find *him* difficult." In an essay published by the *Guardian* last year, she wrote, "I was a riot girl, a do-me feminist, and I posed topless giving the world the finger on the cover of my second book. I have always been the most impossible person ever." Which is exactly what made *Prozac Nation* pitch-perfect for its time. It was a study of the bottomless angst that would later characterize the decade: disappointment in the patriarchal institutions such as academia and publishing, mistrust in popular culture and parental figures, and psychiatric mismanagement. Elizabeth was heralded as the prospective voice of a generation, and then—like other generations' would-be voices—she was taken to task. Reviews called the book solipsistic, even while praising its effervescent prose and refreshing candor.

She had wanted to call it *I Hate Myself and Want to Die*, which feels more apt stylistically, seeing as it is not necessarily focused on Prozac's effects, and it hardly assumes a nation as its scope. In fact, to her detractors, the story was too myopic. As it turns out, though, personal essays could get way more particular, way less self-aware, and still be part of the pop lexicon. Now that we've lived through the advents of tailored streaming services, algorithmic app dating, blogging, vlogging, live computer gaming, and the monetization of personal brands on sponsored sharing platforms, the self-obsessed prodigy has gone mainstream.

"Before *Prozac Nation* came out, people in their twenties didn't write memoirs," Elizabeth reminds me. We're the last two customers in the restaurant. "I think young people were self-reflective, maybe even in writing, but not so much in book form. I spent so much time fighting with people about letting me do that at all. The after-word to the paperback is a defense of writing a memoir. Now I feel like I should take it out. The only reason to leave it in would be to show what a ridiculous world 1995 was, where you had to defend writing a memoir." And now? "The things that get published now are memoirs. This is what happened. I'm horrified by what has happened, because you don't understand how hard it was to convince anybody to give a shit about my anonymous life. I had to explain this to James Frey, who I like. We had this conversation where I had to explain to him what I went through to get them to understand that I did *not* want to write a novel about my life. That was not what I wanted to do. I wanted to *actually* write about my life. I wanted to tell them the truth."

The very next day, I happened to meet with a group of women, writers in their late twenties, all of whom document their own lives publicly—and all of whom had read Elizabeth's latest piece, the one about her father who wasn't really her father. In fact, nonwriters and nonwomen, too, have told me about this essay, apropos of nothing: "Did you read the new Elizabeth Wurtzel story?" amid an era of truly sensational news updates throughout each day. It's a testament to Elizabeth's outlook on writing generously, with an audience in mind. "I don't really need to compare myself to other writers," starts one of the countless nuggets I will take from speaking with her. "I'd rather think, 'Of the things that you could be doing with your time, is this what you want to do? Would you rather be reading what I'm writing or watching a *Law and Order* rerun?'"

Rock, Paper, Scissors

Tech neck, said the page from the *Post*, was exactly what it sounded like. The paper was tattered by rain and dried around a metal gate. This was the first time she had left her apartment in days, to get toilet paper, and still she was being distracted by articles. With her pocketknife, she loosened some edges of the page, but the midsection, the part with the rest of the text, was mulch. This was the dream, she had to remind herself, eyes adjusting to swift movements and crisp colors under the cold sun. She could spend all day in bed, working, wearing her bathrobe or nothing at all, a comforter folded up under her laptop for leverage. Slightly dizzy, she meant to drop the knife back into her pocket but missed. It landed on the sidewalk and a vital hinge ricocheted onto the street, lost forever.

This was what we all wanted, or at least what I wanted, she blinked, backtracking because she had walked past the corner store, her mind a scroll of memes aggregating the all-consuming desire to stay in bed. Every email ping felt like a welcome escape from spelunking through rivals' vacation photos, and yet the email itself was not welcome. Everything was asking her to do something else, to follow up, to make a deadline. Everything was only washed, not actually clean. When she would get flown around for work, the headrests on plane seats were sometimes covered in towel-like cloths, Velcroed on for easy replacement. They were like the bibs for incapacitated people at a home. They only reminded her that there was dirt in her hair, not that the plane was being consistently sanitized of it.

Back in her apartment, she tried to remember if she had taken a bath already that day. On an old sitcom, an out-of-work actor met with his agent in a cluttered office. She had never met her agent in person. She usually woke up late and ordered food from a place around the corner at three so that when the texts about dinner or drinks from friends came flooding in around seven, she would not be tempted by hunger to leave. Something had to happen here. Everyone had told her that she could do a thing.

Once she had a term for it, she knew she had suffered from tech neck day and night. She watched something, she read something, she wrote something, and always her body became a comma. She put her laptop away and read from a book and had the same problem, book neck. If the bed could curl around her like a cocoon, built by doctors with reading in mind, or if the laptop screen could telescope—Whatever happened to the ergonomic keyboards that sloped up in the middle?

She did have a date that night, and so she would have to leave the apartment again. It was with someone she hadn't met yet in person, an online conversation lasting over a week now, someone who she thought was just dangerous enough to be worth sleeping with. A date was really for that purpose alone, seeing as she wouldn't have time for a relationship, and anyway relationships mostly took place in texts.

Her date wanted to tell her about spas. Those imaginary places where furniture exposed to countless human bodies and constant moisture is clean, cleansing, and comfortable. The spas we're used to, she learned, were minimalistic and pseudo-health-centric, as opposed to a parallel tradition of stagey luxury and themed photo opportunities. Certain Korean spas, for example, were much more about eating junk food and taking naps, which feels more honest. Okay, she agreed, because she was on a first date.

For some reason, she lied when asked if she had ever been to a spa. She made up that she'd gone to one with her mother as a child, and then came up with harp music that played while diaphanous curtains parted, tea tree oil and sage smoke clearing her sinuses while steam cleared her pores. The individual rooms were aggressively quiet; the only sounds came from faucets emptying boiling water onto washcloths and shallow pans emptying cold water onto hot rocks. This had to be doing something. Sure. Maybe. It was a fantasy of condensation being so hot and contained it would rid one of toxins. The more impossible it seemed, the more enticing it became.

It's a literal hotbed for germs, was the argument. It's an old-fashioned practice that has no place in modern times. People like the idea that they can pay a third party to relax the body. Relaxation, though, must come from within. That seems obvious. She was drunk now, having only eaten saltines, mustard, and olives that day. Something had to change about her eating habits, but also about her income. She told her date about the bed, how it didn't make sense to get out and it didn't make sense to stay in it, to do work. Sometimes a mailperson or neighbor would knock on her door, and she was annoyed because she was not dressed. Her music was always playing, so they knew she was home, in the late afternoon. It felt wrong that we still had to answer doors.

There is shame in any kind of desire, she said, sure she had not made that up. It was not in service of any point, just a thing that sounded right when she was reminded of the body she'd rather forget. When she worked, it was mostly not working, probably, a wandering day of checking to see if something had happened, abandoning texts she thought she wanted to read, not really masturbating but letting a hand drift toward zones of physical pleasure. There was less of a dirty feeling than a feeling of dirt, layers of waxy grime that dulled her hair and crusted her things.

The conversation grew smaller instead of thicker. In Catherine Breillat's *Anatomy of Hell*, a woman holds up a tampon and says to a man, "See the space it takes up, and one can't even feel it? The same space as most human penises: proof that in intercourse, the act isn't what matters, but its meaning." Still, she would have sex with this person if they wanted her to, because the meaning was in the wanting, sometimes.

The body was never at rest, always spasming toward another position, even though it hardly exercised, maybe *because* it hardly exercised. One arm or a foot would be numb, one finger whiter than the rest, the cold air from a cracked window more titillating than a warm tongue. Inside her coat, the secret of her body twisted and itched, a surface made up of movements.

"Paper, rock, scissors," someone said at the bar, and she watched as two fists smacked onto two open hands. Paper covers rock, but rock breaks scissors, and scissors cut paper. The page from the *Post* had covered a wrought iron fence post and was shredded by an attempt to salvage it with a knife from a multiuse tool. The concrete ground had crushed the usefulness of that tool. It was condensation, though, that had made the text on the page unreadable. Plastic protects everything, she thought, remembering the stack of toilet paper, the replacement knife, and the candy bar she had later bought from the bodega. She had to use the old knife blade to open the packaging surrounding her new one. The chocolate, once out of its wrapper, crumbled between her fingers, chalkier in its joints, obviously old enough to have melted and then re-hardened.

Dates don't organically draw to a close, they have to be ended, and so they had to come up with an end. Do you want to leave? she asked. She could mean to another bar, to her apartment, to respective homes, or anywhere but here. There were so many options, most of them pretty much the same.

Pleasure

"My instant reaction to this is almost too obvious," says Reba, who makes artworks that involve the labor of her submissives. She's responding to my question about societal representations of pleasure, whatever that means these days. "Everything pleasurable will always be increasingly commodified as capitalism and technology excel and therefore become more accessible to consume. The last decade has exploded the possibilities of the purchase of sexual experiences without leaving the bedroom."

She lists cam sessions, private online purchases, social media, and streaming pornography as benchmarks in the history of contemporary desire, the new faces of sex work. We're interested in how pleasure is understood, as a word and as a sensation, after the rise of the attention economy, which generally tends to prioritize anticipation over satisfaction. I'm now used to hearing conversations about the generation currently coming of age (Z) not caring about sex so much. They're at least, apparently, not overwhelmed and obsessed with the idea of it, instead addicted to gamified social interactions.

According to these conversations, Gen Z are even more depressed than the millennials were at their age. That, and they're more aware of and wary of identity politics. Plus, they're relatively numb to advertising. They don't like drugs, driving, or art either, I guess. I've read a few think pieces on this phenomenon that cite studies and statistics, written in the same tone as the ones that used to tell us that kids were having way *too much* sex. I wonder, What happened to turn things around, and at what cost? Have we lost all the inebriated teenage drivers with raging libidos and aspirations of art careers?

"I'm thinking of Lauren Berlant here, when she's talking about romance for women," says Rachel. "Even if these are places of subordination, we can still understand that romance is a place of joy. I am a pessimist about romance and yet, like maybe all of us, romance still has a grip on me." Like Reba, Rachel lets her sex work inform her writing. She's interested in the intersections between sex and money, the fetish, and its object. "I do think that romance, like all things, is tainted by capitalism, and that second-wave feminists were right to criticize romance as the site of women's subordination. But it's not necessary to defend romance in order to understand its pleasures, the euphoria of falling in love. To quote Berlant, 'Everyone knows what the female complaint is: women live for love, and love is the gift that keeps on taking.'"

I wonder, Does an era define the pleasure we feel, or do pleasures we feel define our era? "I like to think about how female body shapes have gone in and out of fashion since I was a teenager," says Reba, "and how many women associate their own sexual pleasure based on how their bodies look. But what was considered hot ten years ago is now outdated. The shape of Victoria Beckham's breasts or Paris Hilton's legs was the epitome of sexuality fifteen years ago, but now appear almost cartoonish in how desexualized they are in relation to Kim Kardashian's alien silhouette. It makes me sad that so many women associate sexual pleasure with their physicality. Neuroticism kills the ability to come."

So much of sex is performative, and performance has lately found new mediums. Perhaps teens are not uninterested in sex but are instead understanding it through other lenses. While everyone's personality becomes a potential cash source, the lines between prostitution and self-promotion are blurred. Sex work is a spectrum, running parallel to newly defined ideas of what constitutes emotional labor.

"There's been a real push amongst escorts to not use the word *escort*," says Rachel, "because it is criminalized and can get our accounts deleted, so terms like *provider* or *companion* have become the norm. But I always liked the word *entertainer*, which is what we use at the strip club and which, to me, has less of a service-industry feel. Of course, because sex work is criminalized, clients retain a lot of power in what our work looks like. If they want us to perform like service industry workers then we all end up performing that work, but I will fight this framing every little chance I get, for my own sanity. Anyway, the lines between performing pleasure and experiencing pleasure get blurred in any kind of sex. Because sex and romance are always mediated by capitalism, we are all actors. It often takes acting to summon up a belief in romance."

The better we know ourselves, we are taught, the better we feel during sex. But that assumes a lot: that our sex lives are mostly within our own control, and that knowing oneself is a gateway to loving oneself. The popularity of roleplay and cosplay during sex is a testament to another theory: maybe the less we are aware of our selfhood, the closer we are to feeling pleasure.

In Atlanta, where one can smoke cigarettes indoors and order a beer for two dollars, I am with mostly couples at the Clermont Lounge. Two of the women, my friends, are very pregnant. Some of the dancers wear sneakers and jean shorts on the bar. Others are in impractical lingerie that gets caught on heeled sandals as they peel every piece of it off.

I love strip clubs, kind of, because they are so diverse in intent and aesthetic, an accidental evaluation of human sexuality, its inexplicable qualities and runaway tangents. In movies, blonde-wigged women in diamante chokers rock back and forth in slow motion, their beauty a thing in and of itself to behold. Men howl while they slap their friends' backs and dozens of dollars explode out of one person's pockets. In a way, this Atlanta club is more like that depiction than most I've seen: people seem happy, even though the dancers are not as young as the ones in the movies, and I heard that in the public bathroom there was an uproar about feces on the floor.

In LA, I show my new boyfriend some favorite spots, including Jumbo's Clown Room. It's his first time at a strip club at all. Some make me miserable, I warn him, and I can never prepare for that feeling because I don't know where it comes from. All strippers look sad in some way, a dancer desperate for singles, walking a fine line between controlling a room and appearing an afterthought. I have no interest in the politics of it, really, only the pure spectacle and its precarity.

I once dated someone who left for a month to assist with an issue of *Playboy's College Girls*. He toured the South, setting up casting calls at big campuses. There was some stipulation that the magazine expressed to readers, I guess, about all the girls in the issue attending a Big Ten school, but the reality, he told me, was that they couldn't scout enough models from even the surrounding community colleges that fit the part. They started in on Hooters and clubs next, first asking women if they were currently in school and then giving up on that, too.

Striptease might be a terrible movie, but it was unfairly reviewed when it came out: the critics wrote that not only was Demi Moore's acting jarringly inconsistent with the overall tone of the film, but her dancing was objectively unsexy. The same was said of *Showgirls*, which ended up a formative image for adolescents at the time. For all our other flaws as a generation, at least we've developed a deeper understanding of what the mere presentation of a sex identity can achieve. Sexiness, like these films, is ridiculous: an imaginary, ephemeral thing, like personal style or the English language. Everyone knows that trying to understand it is in direct competition with appreciating it.

"There was probably a time when I hated the word *pleasure*," says Rachel. "My favorite opening line of any book is from [Georges Bataille's] *Story of the Eye*: 'I grew up very much alone, and as far back as I can recall, frightened of anything sexual.' As a child, I loathed anything sexual, too. I didn't want to see it, didn't want to encounter it. And the word *pleasure* was a word I probably would've encountered in a sexual context, like the name of a strip club on a highway, or the copy on a condom machine, on a late-night phone sex commercial. All of those things draw your eye as a child, the sex industry employing shades of hot pink and lipstick-cursive fonts in their branding. Obviously, this was about, among other things, the ways that sexuality was always presented through a male gaze, the object of sexuality being female and my own assignment as female in life which made me not want to grow up, made me terrified, made me resentful, made me want to disappear."

Rachel's fear of objectification later transformed into something like a desire for it—a common trajectory of fetish. Media plays on fetish, more than anything else, influencing our modes of desire. And since media has changed so much recently, new representations have no doubt started to affect the way younger people, imprinted with their first sexual encounters, desire. A more modular media, on the one hand, gives one the freedom to create one's own version of unfulfilled urges. Binge shopping and binge watching, voyeurism, and exhibitionism of private thoughts enter the arena.

Overstimulation or oversaturation, on the other hand, could possibly be to blame for a reported decrease in sex drives among teenagers. Either way, it is interesting to see the representations of sex and pleasure evolve in a millennial lifetime, from boner-popping beer commercials to the rebranding of sex-positivity, which to my own otherwise socialized brain looks unrelated.

I have no way of proving this, but the increasingly symbolic systems we use to communicate must affect the way we experience pleasure. Interfacing through screens, we use quantifiable points of affirmation, tiny caricatures as reactions, alternative currencies and promises of exposure as payments, and algorithms to discover our friends and lovers.

"If we are non-consensually born into a capitalist system," says Reba, "what could be more taboo than giving money away to an individual without altruistic intent? And instead, the financial dispersal is based on personal masochism. If we cannot exist without the endless need for money, and denial is always a sexual curiosity, it makes sense that some would get pleasure from humiliating themselves through being broke. Especially for men. When there is so much pressure to be the breadwinner, in a world where our value is so often based on the size of our bank accounts, it becomes a form of masochism to give money away."

The erasure of a sex act other than its transactional shell feels thoroughly modern, the plot of science-fictive projection. Pleasure comes from miming work and implying degradation. It is empty of meaning, and its meaninglessness is its allure. The more we assign meaning to symbols, the more we desire the symbols themselves.

The Planet

In an old-timey bar that is surrounded by a flea market in Paris, I watch a lounge singer billed as the flea market's Edith Piaf socialize with regulars, wearing a shirt that says in a repeating pattern "Art is Life," and "No Days Off." Amalia would love this shirt, I think. She would probably love the flea market, and the bar, and the singer, too.

From Paris, I go to Gijón and find myself sitting in the bedroom in which Amalia is staying and also using as part of a film set. This is where she has been sleeping, during the shoot, and it is also the bedroom where her character sleeps. It is covered in photos of Amalia's real cat, Holga, who is in Los Angeles at the time, but makes a cameo in the film via Skype. From this room, I watch the scene Amalia is shooting with her mother, Ale, in the next room. On a director's monitor, Amalia's character comes home after a rough night, has a conversation with her mother, and then, left alone at the kitchen table, begins to cry.

Amalia is directing the scene as well as acting in it, and she wrote it. Her character, Leonor, is a young woman who went to school in London to study fashion (Amalia attended Central Saint Martins) before she ran out of money and turned to escorting as a secret means to fund the rest of her education (Amalia's experience with sex work is publicly ambiguous, but she has addressed its complexities in her art). The character's mother is being played by Amalia's mother. They are in Amalia's hometown, where Ale still lives. The scene plays out, the mother and daughter saying their lines in Spanish. I'm seeing the movie version of a real life, I think— a rare life, maybe, but a real one. The mother leaves. The daughter lets her shoulders slump. She stares vacantly at something, and then winces, the beginnings of tears gathering. I feel like a voyeur, and that feeling builds as time moves on.

On screen, alone, Amalia cries. Jet-lagged and caught off guard, in a tiny room with two strangers, all of us perfectly silent, I am moved to mist. Tears stream down her face and I at first assume they are real, coming from a place of real sadness or exhaustion. Maybe she's looking at some childhood artifact, reminding herself of a shitty upbringing that couldn't have been her fault. She is, after all, visiting a place she left behind. Childhood woes never really go away, and we can summon them for sympathy, for manipulation. "Cut," Amalia says to her crew, in a broken voice.

But then she does the entire scene again, with exactly the same momentum, from start to finish. And then she does it again. And again. Each time, big salty tears streak black eyeliner down her cheeks. "Cut," she says, a final time, but only because the crew needs to eat before all the restaurants close for siesta.

Couched between trips to France and Italy, my first experience in Northern Spain is sentimentalized by its place in my own time-line. The grandeur and crowdedness of more touristy cities give Gijón a diorama-like quality. Its north-pointing beaches lead to a bulb-shaped cliff, a popular lookout point. The waves crashing around it could be inside a bottle. Gijón is large, but its center feels small and old-fashioned, cinematic even if Amalia wasn't filming a feature here—her first, *El Planeta*. Restaurants, stores, and venues feel cosmopolitan, if in a dated sense of the word. At night, the whole city comes out for a walk, a late dinner, and then a coffee with friends. A chlorine-blue skate park on the backside of the cliff is full of teenage boys that don't seem bored. My hotel is next to a casino. All around me, churches and theaters and public artworks tower over subdued conversations. Pairs of older women in matching tweed skirt suits hold one another's arms while shopping on the boulevard or people-watching from benches. This image has come to represent the place, which maybe explains why a particular style is so closely adhered to. Effigies of these colorfully conservative ladies dot the store windows they continuously pass by, a sort of real-life *mise en abyme*.

On the patio of a café, Amalia reminisces about her teenage years. I ask about her father, a tattoo artist who no longer has a shop. She lost contact with him years ago after a painful struggle over assets, she says. He could be here, but she doesn't know for sure. She could run into him, then, I suggest. She doesn't seem worried about that. He's likely in hiding, she says, having evaded many debts, including a large one owed to her. Anyway, Gijón has changed a lot, like most places of a certain size. I try to imagine that this is my hometown. Being here with her is like being in the medium-sized American cities to which I can't fully return because they, too, have changed a little too much. There are glimpses of the familiar that send me to another time, a time when, in retrospect, a place belonged to me: a scuffed window and the faded bottles behind it; a bus station that looks abandoned but isn't; the carpeted, wood-paneled apartment that I've never seen before but is more like home than home is, now.

Before I was in Paris, I was in New Orleans for a wedding, and before that, New York, where I live. Gijón is far from sleepy, but in comparison to these places, it is quaint. Consistently grey skies drain the area of color and sharpen its focus. This contrast comes alive in *El Planeta*, which Amalia films in black and white. The choice unhooks the narrative from a particular period, in keeping with so many small anachronisms found here.

I have dinner with Nacho, who plays a john in *El Planeta*. I talk him into one drink, since I want to try the cider for which Asturias is known. There is a trick to pouring it from an absurd distance, letting it aerate on its way into the glass. Nacho is recognized by a fan in the restaurant who knows him as the host of Turner Classic Movies Spain's monster series, among other things. He tells me he hates working in Los Angeles because it is like a giant parking lot—kind of why I love it, I say. Even the landmarks look like afterthoughts there, wedged into corners made by wide, curving freeways and seen from a car window. I am reminded that this is where Amalia lives, now, which doesn't seem quite right. She is a famous artist, not a Hollywood wannabe, but now that she has become an actor and a filmmaker, she is moving to New York.

All of Amalia's art projects run the risk of not be taken seriously, since *Excellences & Perfections* (2014), the one that put her on the map, was based on a pseudo-truth: on social media, Amalia developed a fiction, in which she played a character. This character, a sugar baby, played a role, too, as any sex worker, influencer, and/or gold digger does. She, the character, created a fantasy for an off-screen benefactor, a man understood to be funding her life. As this character shopped and traveled and self-medicated, she created a fantasy in which an audience of strangers could participate.

Through this enactment, Amalia says she found plenty of insight—about art, about identity, about expectation. Every lie revealed a new truth. Later, after her followers discovered that she was not a blonde with augmented breasts, the reactions ranged from impressed to angry. After that, Amalia's projects were understandably questioned by critics: Was she really bringing a pet pigeon to an office? Was she actually on the cover of a fashion magazine? Was that even really her, taking pole dancing lessons after a car accident left her legs in chronic pain? The images of her own face covered in viscous liquid at red carpet events were surely made in Photoshop, but who could be sure?

I walk past El Planeta, the movie's eponymous waterfront restaurant, which is littered with teenagers leaning on steps, holding skateboards, maybe making plans for the night, but more likely settling into this spot, a perfect perch from which to watch the rest of the city. In Amalia's scenes, worlds develop within worlds, and "The Planet" takes on a few meanings. Places and identities collide and collapse into one another, obscuring and then revealing their individual pulls.

Hollywood

Once Upon a Time... in Hollywood (2019) centers on two male characters, sidelining the action of the Manson murders in the same way the women in the real Manson plot must have felt sidelined. I'm struck by that particular sensitivity: women are not brought into a conversation easily. They are watched from afar or they are too close for comfort. The men, unsure of how to handle, say, an unhappy wife, a precocious child actress, or a conniving teen runaway, resort to brute force. They take easy ways out. They exercise the privileges with which they were born, and for which the world has cherished them.

The idea that a film could romanticize the nostalgia we have for a past romanticization (poking holes in it along the way) is maybe obnoxiously high-concept. To me, this is a movie about the way we see an era from outside of it. It's a movie about women: the sex symbol Sharon Tate, about whom the world knew very little until she was murdered while pregnant and married to Roman Polanski; and the brainwashed women in Charles Manson's cult, about whom the world knew even less, until they murdered a few people, including Sharon Tate. It's also a movie about the machine that created these archetypes and the men who were cogs in it, with the best and the worst intentions. It's about Hollywood, once upon a time, if that wasn't obvious.

When Laura Mulvey wrote about cinematic male gazes, or when, later, Alison Bechdel wrote about peripheral female characters, it wasn't to say that these ogling, excluding movies are bad. Each theorist clearly reveres the canon while she criticizes the culture that has created it: with men in control of our industries, our governments, and our fears, they are in control of our narratives, too, both fictional and not. Movies written and directed by women often don't pass the Bechdel Test, either. These essays mean to measure our own everyday psychologies, questioning the ways we imagine gender.

In epics and fairy tales, the savior is a man, but sometimes, so is the villain. Women are central but usually dependent: someone to be rescued, a beacon, an idol, a voiceless beauty, an angel on one shoulder, a devil on the other. There is an argument that women are simply accessories to a plot if they do not drive it. Perhaps women in old films are more props than persons, but that is only if you consider helplessness the same thing as lacking agency. I see the Sharon Tate character in *Once Upon a Time... in Hollywood* as fan fiction based on true circumstances. Like Marilyn Monroe, Tate was married to a serious writer but not quite taken seriously. She was gazed upon more than she was listened to. She must have had a complicated relationship to that gaze. In Quentin Tarantino's take, Sharon is often alone. She wanders into a movie theater playing one of her features, attempting to understand the gaze, watching others watch her.

Sharon Tate apparently gave Roman Polanski the Thomas Hardy novel *Tess of the d'Urbervilles: A Pure Woman Faithfully Presented* (1891). It inspired him to write and direct an adaptation, his award-winning *Tess*, dedicated to his late wife. She had hoped to star in *Tess*, the story goes, but just after giving him the book to read, she was killed. (Nastassja Kinski was cast instead.) This anecdote about a woman hoping to exist through her husband's narrative—about an actress enjoying a book about a fictional woman's tragic life and handing it to a director so he can recreate that life, just for her—is topped off by the murder. The story of Sharon Tate could have the same subtitle as *Tess*.

In one scene, Margot Robbie's Sharon buys a first edition of *Tess* at a bookstore for her husband, who, she says, will love it. This isn't a scene that passes the Bechdel Test, since it does not include women talking to one another about something other than a man. In fact, the store clerk is a man. But in another scene, at the movie theater, Sharon talks to a ticket saleswoman about the movie—the one she's in, *The Wrecking Crew*. Yes, that's her, the actress from *Valley of the Dolls*. They talk for a while. The joke is that the woman doesn't recognize the actress because the picture on the marquis is of the real Sharon Tate, not Margot Robbie as Sharon Tate. Here are two women talking about something other than a man, and what they are discussing is the person for which one of these women is a proxy. This is me, she insists, pointing to a poster.

In genre films, women are unhappy, desperate, and dying to transcend. Their lives are impossible to rearrange. One could either give in by choosing another man to follow, or give up and be sad, forever. In her real life, Sharon Tate chose movie stardom, putting her life in the hands of producers, directors, her husband, and eventually, accidentally, Charles Manson. Marilyn Monroe chose men, too. Each have become icons of an era, the perfect encapsulation of what was beautiful and wrong with a world that wanted them so much, it wouldn't let them live.

Anyway, the movie is about men, mostly. It's about Los Angelenos who traffic in violence, and who are fun to watch. It's about violence against women, violence against men, violence perpetuated by movies, and the violence we feel inside of us, perhaps due to the unfairness of representation, as one Manson girl suggests in much more hippie terms. It's the movies that made us this way, but really, it's us that made the movies that way, in which women are quietly happy when they're alone or uncomfortable and bitter when they're forced to recognize their own positions, in which they speak about men, or they don't speak at all.

When the movie ends, I watch the credits, which are full of women: choreography Toni Basil, stunts Zoë Bell, costumes Arianne Phillips. The Manson girls are partially Hollywood royalty, the daughters of Kevin Smith, Uma Thurman and Ethan Hawke, and Andie MacDowell. Cameos by Lena Dunham, Robert De Niro, Bruce Dern, and Luke Perry are maybe unnecessary but feel right given the subject matter. The casting feels, like so many other elements of the movie, anachronistic and meta, driving us to make connections between then and now, the hierarchy of Hollywood and an age of ignorance.

The ending is unexpected. Remember in *Django Unchained*, when there was an ahistorical slave uprising, and in *Inglourious Basterds*, when Adolf Hitler was killed? These fantasies construe an obsession with cinema—what it was supposed to be able to do, and how it ended up failing. What if movies could re-mythologize history, turning the tables to favor the oppressed, in a madcap adventure? This one, too, changes history to make the good guys win. Isn't that what you wanted?

The Wheel

A sign of the times, Staten Island's 630-foot waterfront Ferris wheel was scheduled to go up in the early 2010s. Now, as the decade comes to a close, production has been paused, like with so many other ideas we dreamed up ten years ago. The New York Wheel, meant to draw tourists down from Manhattan, lacked private funding. In 2018, it was officially cancelled (after investors had spent a reported $400 million). Like the London Eye, Roue de Paris, and Santa Monica's Pacific Wheel, it would be a skyline-diversifying attraction. In theory, it was going to connect an overlooked borough to the rest of New York. From atop a ride that slow and high, one can really romanticize a city. But looking back on the '10s, what it once promised now seems impossible, an ambition reduced to its scrapped and un-scrappable parts, a pile of trash in the former home of the world's largest landfill.

The failure of the Ferris wheel project, according to some people who are protective of Staten Island's autonomy, is metaphorical, an eye never opening toward the city. A friend there told me that the Wheel, like a band he named after it, was finished before it started. And as with a planned Amazon Long Island City headquarters that was shut down by protesters before breaking ground, the reality of New York came into focus with this un-development: the city known for rapid change will keep things the same if it can help it.

On the other hand, retail concepts are opening here all the time, like those in the "largest mixed-use private real estate venture in American history," Hudson Yards. This year, the *New York Times* described the new set of skyscrapers as endlessly bleak. It's true, all these new malls fitted with residential and office spaces and surrounded by modern walkways that can transform a bike path into a selfie destination subscribe to an unfamiliar dream of shitting where one eats and never leaving the stench of one's waste—a logical step after our subjectivities have become so intertwined with shopping and selling. New, city-like malls are popular all over the Eastern world already, offering complete lifestyles fully built within a corporate identity. It's like an updated Vegas Strip but without the casinos—like Instagram, but with the necessary nourishment of food and shelter. It's also like a mockery of human existence, a giant ant farm. Whether you're purchasing, ingesting, or just taking it in, you're always consuming.

Malls are a way of being inside culture while being protected from it, a space for vapidity to breed community. The return of the mall has been predicted for decades, but it might only make sense starting now in America, with screen fatigue leading us away from our social media, but not all the way out of a consumer loop. Aside from these complexes, an emblem of the '10s might be the video screens that now litter New York City in place of wheat-pasted posters, rendering every available corner a potential successor to Times Square. We're living in the future, in the year that both *Blade Runner* and *Akira* were set, while falling in love with artists' animatronics, poetic bots, and a new crop of CGI influencers.

Speaking with a high school teacher, I am informed that the political correctness rumored to riddle the youth is, in her New York City classroom, met with nihilism, and even though everything has changed, things have basically stayed the same there, too. Whenever I'm around them, I try to ask the children of tomorrow what their thoughts are on today, hoping to hear a firsthand account of what it feels like to live in a world in which everything is a marketing ploy, but interviewing kids about their predictions for the next decade feels like asking the patient for a prognosis. What we've experienced aesthetically in this decade mostly comes from the analysis of information prepared by *the youth*: the rise and fall of millennial pink, to be replaced by its color wheel opposite, Z-foam green (I made that up); a proliferation of content appealing to our crippling, constant anxieties; corporate advertising's taking on the meme structure; and the relentless marketing of easier, app-accessible options for the at-home binger of absolutely everything. The culture is branded in layers like a regenerating epidermis, and it is pretending to be more like a mirrored surface, reflecting the beholder, or at least their attention-spending habits.

But perhaps no trend defines the '10s as well as the magic trick people can perform by holding two truths to be self-evident simultaneously. By this I mean conflicting opinions coming from one mind, and that mind earnestly believing each. We live in a time when the term *transgender*—the roots of which rely on the concept of a gender binary—is often lumped together with the term *nonbinary*, the conceit of which suggests that a gender binary is irrelevant. Linguistically, these ideas are in opposition, yet the popular belief is that one can "be" nonbinary and "support" transgender rights (which is, in practice, true). A paradox: The belief that gender is a spectrum, not a hard-lined division based on sex organs, would propose that adhering to a set of systematically oppressive stereotypes—which would include feminization tactics like cosmetic surgeries—is counterproductive. We also live in a time when many of us know from experience that these stereotyping tactics do feel productive in some cases, adding to a spectrum of identity rather than mimicking an outdated definition of it.

That opposing truths can exist in one hive mind is unsettling, though. Clearly, it's not only the people who require the sort of galaxy brain to understand the contradictions of gender-fucking and gender-reifying lumped into one acronym who end up experiencing a dysmorphic existence. And this paradox has led us, it seems, to an impasse that textures the decade.

Or maybe that was the chicken before the egg. Maybe the multiverse of opposing truths held by the younger generation was inspired by so many conflicting data sets proving the same point, so much well-meaning momentum leading to opposing conclusions, the hypocrisy of a grassroots political movement becoming a stage for consumerism, along with a United States cabinet known for bending the truth and then bending it back.

Picture the phrase *all genders bathroom* appearing beneath that symbol of a dress-wearing figure conjoined with a pants-wearing figure. Not only does the symbol point to its own fallacy (there are only two "genders" here, or maybe one, in the process of changing clothes), but it asks us to continue utilizing a system of design that paints women as dress-wearers and men as pants-wearers, a comically dated code in this context. Plus, we've had single-stall all-genders bathrooms this whole time without labeling them. Multi-stall bathrooms, on the other hand, have created, before the term was heavily in use, a "safe space" for women by assigning men their own rooms, or a "boys' club" for urinal users, depending on your perspective. The stalled spaces that have transitioned to genderlessness cause a mix of emotions: this is what we wanted, right? Yes and no, because both yes and no are possible to feel at once. If bathrooms, the historically politicized spaces, were once more segregated than they are now, we can assume progress has been made, but simultaneously, it is easy to imagine a world wherein, if bathrooms had never been divided into genders, there would be a movement to suggest that they should be.

Contradictions in social lessons aren't specific to Generation Z, of course. When Generation Y were kids in the '90s, we were told by a whitened Michael Jackson that "it don't matter if you're black or white," for example. On top of the confusing messenger, the song's message complicated ideas of cultural preservation by mixing it with rhetoric for cultural erasure—the multicultural faces of the song's music video, some invented digitally, illustrate an entirely different ideal than today's progressivism. Back then, the term *appropriation* was linked to a nebulous idea of culture after it was more popularly used to describe what happens to art, and then a type of art. An appropriation artist's work shifts attention to the money aspect of the job: What is something worth, if it is simply the artist putting his name on something that isn't his? That the content of the work is stolen, transposed, or crassly commodified calls into question ideas of integrity. *Cultural appropriation*, on the other hand, a buzzy phrase of the past decade, subverts another kind of value, sometimes described as "credit" that is "due." Within systems that have subjected minority groups to the very actions that suppress them, the concept that credit can be subverted or reverted is a tricky one, however simplified it has become in call-outs. There are created capitals within oppressive systems—attention, comfort, money, acclaim—and it is at once understandable and foolish to petition for these things.

Fashion, another type of credit, used to be much less precious about value than art, seeing as it always admitted to being commercial. Everything we wear is an appropriation. The very act of designing a garment today is acquiescing to this standard. Cultural appropriation can be used to describe all fashion, if read as a simple combination of words with individual meanings. Everything we wear must come from somewhere, and the idea that some items of clothing are culture-free, that they are the blank catalyst for an inoffensive new custom, is similar in its whitewashed outlook to the categorization of the majority and its others. Is a T-shirt more basic than a sari? Does it matter who is making it? Basic Western collars are derived from the traditional dresses of Eastern cultures: the mandarin collar came from the Manchu, the halter top from a Vietnamese yếm.

Imagine if only the people who could prove an affiliation with a cloth's cut were allowed to design or wear it. I am picturing the opening act of a Miss Universe pageant. Or imagine if everyone wore a uniform issued by a world government. Fashion was invented to expose the differences between ethnic groups and classes. It historically separated tribes, marked family lineages, rewarded royal blood, and stratified the wealthy. Now, it is a tool used to accelerate consumerism by putting pressure on a calendar, segmenting and sub-segmenting time periods into shopping cycles. It is a language that one must relearn every few months. Like memes or celebrity gossip, it invents ways to evaluate its beholder. Fashion today is less about proving status than it is about signaling involvement in conversations concerning values, seduction, education, sophistication.

The '10s were, maybe most of all, about finding ways around appropriation by rejecting all sensitive cultural indicators via sponsored personal branding. Commercialism has birthed its own subcultures that are decentered, detached, and immune to guilt. Marketing is an aesthetic, too, and it can be worn in creative ways. The New York Wheel and the Amazon HQ weren't built, but plenty of branded experiences existed in this decade, all of them conflating romance with consumerism, killing the two birds of tourism and marketing with one stone. If a so-called Instagrammable environment—say, a selfie room created for a sponsored experience by an agency hired by a corporation in one of these new malls—attracts lines of people hungry for interaction and exposure, and its valuelessness becomes exponentially valuable in the attention economy, is it not a feat of art and architecture?

It is at least an answer to the anxiety over appropriation and ownership. The necessary brandlessness of a photo op and the necessary branding of a step-and-repeat are no longer competing, the signifiers working in tandem to create a loop of destabilized responsibility. The view from a Ferris wheel is not as prized as a well-lit photo booth, the branding of which is a bonus, a plot point in one's projected narrative. The combination of the self, the selfie, and the selfie space is a mirror turned in on itself, advertising to an audience of active influencers. The art here is the absence of culture—and it goes viral, mutually benefiting both parties. It is appropriation culture—the space for branding, personal and otherwise to take place, at once an absence and a substance.

The Cave

"The most important thing is that this is a project with meaning, that we do something more than make money," Roth is saying. He's just Roth, founder of Roth Architecture and a self-described *visionary*. "The idea is to get out of the cave." This is a reference, I think, to the tunnel vision inflicting our human race, or, as Roth calls us, "the human tribe." We're in his Tulum home, which looks like a climbing/skate park, or a lived-in lunar-surface movie set, in a jungle. Chet Baker's voice wafts over lily pads as we sit down in a concrete nest surrounded by manmade waterfalls to have lunch on latticed ceramic. The plates, designed by Roth's chef, are more like upside-down bowls, lacy pedestals holding bouquets of ceviche.

It's my second day in Mexico, and visiting Roth's place is somewhat climactic, even after touring his other bizarre properties. Approaching what looks like a literal hole in a wall, we're led around curving corners into open closets, over embedded floor bookshelves, into the chandeliered shower. Chopin's Nocturne in E-flat Major mysteriously floods the space as we notice netted hammocks and a baby grand piano under a strange red glow. The house itself is hidden behind Roth's Museion gallery, a concrete building that spirals around preexisting trees. The gallery's curator joins us for lunch, as does one of her new artists. He will be, she explains, the first exhibitor in her event program at Roth's other gallery, Sceno, which is connected to his beachfront resort Azulik, which opened in 2018.

Over charred whitefish steak, Roth describes tentative plans for new ways of living and commuting in places currently encumbered by climate crises. His goal is to get people to be more aware of their surroundings by stepping into, or even just seeing images of, his fantastic architecture. His ideas are acutely influenced by ayahuasca ceremonies. I've heard that he has participated in more than one hundred.

"Technology alone won't be the solution," he says, although drones may be a big part of his next project, the details of which are under development. Luxury travel, of course, won't solve anything either, but Azulik is different: "We're the second-most followed hotel on Instagram," he says, when I ask him about its typical clientele. "Only point three percent of them can come, but these people are interested in our project."

The doctrine *If you build it, they will come* has been replaced by the approach *If they are coming, we should build it*. These structures are, I am told, erected without blueprints by Indigenous Mayan craftsmen atop a network of outlines that account for the earth's natural surface and attributes, elevated so as not to disturb the jungle floor. Most of us are inured to the cries of "sustainability" when it comes to art events. After all, what could be less eco-sensitive than a temporary, large-scale attraction that boosts international travel and requires ad hoc production? Putting ironies aside, though, as luxury resort/nightclub/galleries go, Azulik and Sceno are at least remarkable for their intentions of coexisting with coastal Mexico. The rooms at Azulik, for example, are not air conditioned or illuminated electrically. Instead, candles are lit each evening and small battery-powered fans spin over circular beds curtained with cheesecloth. There are no showers, only (scalding hot) baths, and the individual hot tubs on each beachfront balcony must be filled manually (meaning the water is cold by the time we get in). The presence of raccoons and large iguanas proves that the wildlife has not been completely run out from under the hotel.

That said, the strip on which Azulik is situated was already crowded with other resorts, clubs, and restaurants guarded by armed security before 2018. Beachwear boutiques and pharmacies between the attractions stay open late here, and everything is overpriced, even by New York standards. Azulik is one of the most expensive resorts on the strip, intended as an oasis inside a destroyed oasis, a magical bridge from the paved-over paradise that originally brought the business here. The floors are made of thick wooden vines laid straight, each of them hammered down with hundreds of tiny nails.

I happen to arrive in Tulum amid a massive festival called Day Zero (something a cenote tour guide tells me may have killed several jaguars last year by scaring them out of their habitat and onto the freeway with its loud bass music). As I'm carted around to snorkel near alligators and bats, throngs of people in impractical techno-fest attire gather in the sun, their airbrushed faces running and their felt hats damp.

My first night here, I meet the curator, her new artist, and a publicist in one of the four candlelit restaurants at Azulik. Our reserved table isn't ready. Whenever one of us asks about dinner, the curator tells us to relax and take some tequila shots. Over an hour later, we are seated.

"So," says the artist, "what is art?"

The curator groans, then launches into her life story. "This was before we got into our *The Sorrows of Young Werther* phase and tried to commit suicide in the forest," she laughs. "I grew up five minutes from the forest where the Brothers Grimm were born, in a monastery."

"That's a heavy vibe," says the artist.

"Yeah. Then I became a lawyer. For six years, in Paris and New York. Corporate." Next, she says, she became interested in art, and the partners at her firm let her go on sabbatical. "One of the partners was especially understanding. He was a novelist."

"Lawyers are always writing books," says the publicist.

"Well, what is law? It's a fiction. When I left my law firm I went to Christie's Education. It was a good class, but it was a lot of work. I had hoped for less work."

"That's why most people get into art," says the artist.

The next day, I visit Museion, where the curator gives me a tour of the space's current exhibition. Descending the spiral walkway, she recognizes a friend, who is there with some English speakers. One, a woman wearing a fan of feathers behind one ear, a feathered necklace, and a gown attached to each of her middle fingers with rings, is working on an environmental project of her own, she explains. Her friend wears a gold snake around one hand, a crystal pendant on a leather strap, and a Louis Vuitton purse.

The exhibition includes a rub-and-sniff pile of wooden blocks in the shape of their scents' molecules, which belong to a species of seaweed growing in unprecedented amounts on the Mayan Riviera coastline, and a video featuring a cephalopod inhabiting a 3D-printed shell. The curator introduces her new artist to the group, mentioning his upcoming "interspecies" concert at Sceno: "They connect sensors to plants to capture their biorhythms, which then translates into music."

"I've heard it," says one guest. "I've seen the videos. It's so beautiful. It's wow. It's wow. The whole concept is wow." We are all encouraged to join the guided meditation and breathwork classes with these sensor-connected plants, which react to the room's changing energies. Later, at the workshop, we are told in no uncertain terms that the music we are hearing is not made by the plants. Sensors feed information to a software program and musicians choose what sounds come out. The sensors only guide the persistence of these sounds, then, once they are inputted. Basically, the droning quality of the music is all that can be attributed to the potted flora that surrounds us (hung in pretty baskets handmade by a group of Indigenous teenagers determined to live off the land surrounding Roth's buildings).

The first thing one notices about Azulik is that it is photogenic; its wooden bench swings over pools over the marble-green ocean make for world class selfies. Sitting on a lobby swing that got better Wi-Fi than my room, I watched at least a half dozen women wearing some bangle-y, semitranslucent outfit lead personal photographers around the stilted walkways. If it weren't for their light gray contacts and dimensionalizing, shimmery makeup, I am sure I would have mistaken them for costumed dancers readying to perform some traditional ritual about which I had yet to learn. I wonder how they feel about the rudimentary bathing situation, the waterless toilet, and the overall lack of privacy in our round, curtainless, open plan rooms, which is put into sharp relief when I notice a man peering in at me while I am changing into a swimsuit.

My last night in Tulum, I attend the interspecies concert, which features a human singer and another human guitarist. They riff, the singer chanting about "peace" and "plants," mostly. Presumably, our energy was being measured by vines and bromeliads. I spot Roth, who, like most of the guests, ends up horizontal on cushions laid out for the audience. I'm pretty sure I see the woman with the Louis Vuitton purse from before, and remember something Roth said about paying attention to the jungle's music instead of to the whims of capitalism: "It's so simple. We say yes, yes, yes, but now we go to the store, and we buy Louis Vuitton and live in an apartment of marble, isolated."

On a Xanax I'd bought legally at the pharmacy down the street, I try to listen to the music of the gallery (underneath Azulik's own pulsing nightclub)—a mix of sounds created by an algorithm controlled by polygraphs attached to leaves and live musicians—and instead can only see my immediate surroundings: a hotel on the beach, with a Dior gift shop at the front.

Apocalypse

In late 2019, at a screening of the documentary *Martin Margiela: In His Own Words*, fashion theorist Li Edelkoort lamented the direction in which fashion has gone since Margiela stopped designing. No one is trying to be anonymous like he was, in an age of the fame-hungry creative director, she hissed, after summoning a moment of silence for ex-Balenciaga designer Josephus Thimister, who had committed suicide that week. Another ex-Balenciaga designer, the currently sponconning Alexander Wang, happened to be sitting in the front row.

In the weeks before New York Fashion Week Fall/Winter 2020 rolled to a simmer, the so-called retail apocalypse was swiftly adding names to its list. The typical news items about New York hot spot turnovers—B Bar, City Bakery—came with an added sting, sitting in between stories about Macy's, Forever 21, Fairway, Bed Bath & Beyond, and Walgreens shuttering multiple locations.

January had been a month of award shows, and maybe the most outrageous fashion moment among them was the 30%-off Dillard's dress Lana Del Rey wore to the Grammys, supposedly a last-minute idea that happened while visiting a local mall (this, after the singer had starred in several Gucci campaigns). And speaking of malls, Hudson Yards' "Vessel"—a massive, walkable sculpture many have nicknamed the "Shawarma" due to its chiseled, conical shape—was the site of a teen suicide the first day of February, subsequently redefining a destination erected in part to attempt retail revitalization.

Then, Opening Ceremony said it would be closing, too. The bulletin came just before one explaining that over in Paris, the Jean Paul Gaultier couture show about to happen would be the designer's grand finale. Tom Ford opted to show in Los Angeles during NYFW again this season, to coincide with the Oscars. Ralph Lauren, Tommy Hilfiger, and Wang opted out of this one, too (all showing at other dates and locations).

One fashion show I attended was a full-on musical about the retail apocalypse, performed by professionals dressed up as large versions of the designer's bags. It opened at eleven in the morning and again at noon in the basement of a downtown hotel and was sponsored by Ketel One Vodka, Kettle chips, St. Ives, Vans, Milk Bar, and a type of green juice shot. One of the bags was displayed in a giant cube of ice surrounded by cut wildflowers and halved papaya. An oversized version of another bag spun from the ceiling like a mirror ball. On stage, a saxophonist played standards until the seventeen performers cast in this twenty-minute double matinee took their places.

Within a *Wizard of Oz*–inspired plotline, the beaded bag-designer protagonist's dream isn't to go home, but to open a store in SoHo. "What I really want," she sings, "is a shop of my own on Prince or Spring or Grand." Shaking her head at Brooklyn neighborhood suggestions, she meets up with a Wicked Witch–like landlord on Prince Street. "Everything is closing here," the landlord warns her, "from Barneys to freaking Payless. Now Dean & DeLuca's gone, and the yuppies are in fucking distress." The story goes off the rails after that. A stray dog puppet convinces the disheartened designer that her store will be the best of the upscale neighborhood, because it was always her dream to open it: "Like Frida Kahlo painting in a body cast, like Greta Thunberg on a BBC broadcast … nothing can dim the light within us," then a chant spelling out the designer's name, and a medley with the full cast. The guy dressed as a martini-shaped bag is holding a liter of Ketel One.

Throughout this fashion week, members of Extinction Rebellion dressed in upcycled materials staged protests, demanding transparency and sustainability in the industry. The atmospheres of each show I attended felt increasingly dark: a runway in an old library that ended in the shadowy stacks; a scuffed Plexiglas box inside of which models writhed. It seemed impossible that one show's location, a closed Abercrombie & Fitch store, wasn't a nod toward today's shopping landscape.

"We won't be showing this NYFW," said a post on a prominent New York label's Instagram. "There's a lot going on in our world right now, and not everything can be solved with fashion." I DMed the designer, and she told me she was in New Hampshire volunteering for Bernie Sanders ahead of the Democratic primary. "It's okay to make clothes about being anxious and sad but at some point, it's like, 'Why am I putting energy toward that?' I needed to put that energy elsewhere."

Some of the shows I saw were pretty anxious, like the one accompanied by a live band of teenagers playing covers of songs by Weezer, Nirvana, and Yeah Yeah Yeahs. Many were choreographed or acted, rather than simply walked, like the one-act play at Sotheby's to promote a Samsung partnership, in which sixteen models sat at sixteen typewriters and didn't accidentally generate a Shakespearean text. "I'm not ready," said sixteen voices in several languages over a loudspeaker as each model answered an as-yet-unavailable folding-screen smartphone.

"What I love about her is she has this alchemy," said a former Olympic swimmer at La Mercerie. "Her art form lends itself to people who not only do things, but do really powerful, impactful things." The swimmer was referring to the time her wife, the United Nations program coordinator for an LGBT rights group, wore one of the designer's dresses at the UN Open Debate on Women, Peace, and Security. "The idea for this salon was born of that moment," the swimmer explained, mentioning a few of the night's politically minded speakers. I had thought I was attending a fashion show.

We, the guests, were seated at long, candlelit tables and served a three-course meal. At the front of the room, Justin Vivian Bond sang "a very obvious choice," Carly Simon's "You're So Vain," before the mic was opened to impromptu wedding-like speeches about the designer. "This is all her, actually, that I bought myself," said Molly Ringwald. Sitting next to me, Debbie Harry expressed admiration for the collection as it was walked out around our table. Almost under her breath, she said she especially liked the silver spoon chokers. Michael Stipe recalled how he used to wear the designer's clothing himself, back when she designed menswear. "He'd get it at Opening Ceremony," said the musician's boyfriend, raising an eyebrow.

Over dinner, topics ranged from the ketamine revival to raising teen twins. Alex Auder, who described herself as "some yoga instructor who lives in Philadelphia," mentioned being asked to do a guided relaxation that evening, but only if "it felt right." As dessert arrived, she took the microphone and began with a steadied, lowered voice: "I invite you to take part in this neoliberal meditation manifestation. Allow yourself to let go, into the clingy hand of the free market. Do you feel it?"

"No," answered Debbie Harry.

"I feel it," said Cindy Sherman, arms raised.

"You are now dissolving into little bits of human capital. Visualize green, from your consciousness—that is, in your head—

trickling down into your pelvic bowl. Watch out! You might become incontinent. Don't worry. It's all an illusion. It actually trickles back up, ha, ha, ha. And that is how the State works." Eventually, a countdown to snap out of our trance ended in an a cappella rendition of the late-'70s Enjoli 8-Hour Perfume jingle ("I can bring home the bacon, fry it up in a pan, and never, never let you forget you're a man, 'cuz I'm a woman, Enjoli").

On Saturday at Dover Street Market, it was difficult to tell if a show was even happening. No runway had been marked off for the secret presentation that had been discreetly announced to friends of the designers via text. We might have been trolled, guests joked, clutching glasses of white wine through the store's mazy levels. Suddenly, eighteen models holding numbered cards like those used in early couture presentations were speed-walking by. As soon as I could take in a sequined tuxedo jacket, the show was apparently over. Someone tried to exit through the wrong door and a fire alarm sounded, but no one evacuated before finishing their free drinks. "The collection," the designer later told me, "is about dead ends, feeling burned-out and destroyed, and the coping mechanisms one uses to deal with disaster."

An older label opted to forego a runway in favor of exhibiting look-book prints at its store. The opening was packed. Everyone around me kept asking, "Is something else going to happen here?" Posters were handed out at the exit. At an actual, traditional show, guests discussed the downward slide of the NYFW schedule. "I have, like, one show a day," said a London editor. During an after-party at the Dance, models and drag queens urged guests to take the stage, only so they could be ushered off by a security guard while Avril Lavigne's "What the Hell" played. At the bar, a stranger sidled up and offered a scoop: this would likely be the last fashion week party at the venue. "Bottle service," he sneered about the alleged new ownership.

On Monday, looking at the show notes for a presentation, a guest pointed at model Alexandra Marzella's name, whispering, "I knew we'd see pregnant Ally all over this fashion week." She emerged in a transparent bodysuit and dragonfly wings, and I was reminded of the last scene of *Ready to Wear*, in which a pregnant model walks the runway wearing only a bridal veil. The whole week was, in retrospect, a little like watching the fashion show scene from a movie, a joke about the unwearableness of conceptual clothes. But that nude model (the finale after a parade of nude models) in the Robert Altman film wasn't meant to be cynical or even scandalous. As the fictional designer Simone Lo says, in a runway voiceover, "For me, it's the closing of a circle and the beginning of something new. Something new. New. New."

Part II

New York, 2020

This could be my undoing, but I'm getting a lot done. I believe I share that sentiment with a few of us whose jobs went from an office to online. Coming up with tag lines is a weird balance between addressing relevant topics and attempting relevance, which in the end can feel as slippery as writing poetry, but whenever some overwhelming, ubiquitous issue creates a current of new meanings, writing copy gets murkier: words float upward or get sucked downward, depending on what associations can be read into them, and nothing sounds as prescient as it would have a few months ago. Communications with friends and acquaintances have become loaded. The crisis is so complex and far-reaching, I don't find avoiding it possible. But others disagree. The problem is that I'm listing grievances but not solutions. Why, I ask, should I know the answers?

Most ideas are bad, as an economist on the radio says. I've heard this era described as a tangible end to collective anxiety, the brink of an unfathomable catastrophe, and a cold war. I have to admit that I get a thrill every time Amy Goodman says she's reporting from the epicenter of the crisis, New York City, my city.

I think about physical spaces that might disappear. I first met my boyfriend at a sweaty basement party. I've never had so much fun as when I am on a plane in business class, or a boat with my friends, or in a hotel room alone. Time is moving incredibly quickly now, like a storm after the sky was swelling ominously for years.

Still, people are bored by the new breakneck pace of life because it is happening to each of us in isolation if we can afford it. I have become aware that some people do not find hourly calamity updates impressive, and that I have little in common with these people. The system is rigged. Money isn't real. Self-care isn't healthcare. The maxim "stay home" is grating to those who once had valid reasons for spending as much time away from home as possible.

Frank Sinatra's "New York, New York" is played out of many windows here at seven o'clock, when the city applauds the essential workers every day. I much prefer the Liza Minnelli version, from the movie *New York, New York*, which came first, and which holds in itself all the blind passion and wavering denial needed to "make it there" at the time it was sung (in the '70s, but for a story set in the '40s), when New York was considered far more dangerous. In the film, Liza's character eventually writes the song "New York, New York," an overly confident ode to a city that isn't doing much for her at the time. The flat scenery and superdimensional acting intensify the film's themes of show business's empty promises, of life's highs and lows harmonizing.

My own childhood was spent in theaters and the companies that ran them—quiet worlds hung with paintings that looked abstract at close range, shadowy, windowless places, cool and covered in velvet or muslin. Massive rigs strung with ropes and cables lurched while people wearing all black cursed, camouflaged in darkness. I saw the work that went into putting actors on stage, the ugliness of opera singers' makeup and of ballet dancers' throbbing feet, not a glittery rush of giggling chorus girls. Everything felt at once hushed and loud as my sister and I wandered the front and back of house. And then it was curtains up, and everything would fall into place, except it was all being wrestled there with braided metal cords.

I love musicals about show business because they are always sad. The theater can't save you; it is something there for you to save, a mouth that begs to be fed. As a metaphor, it works for me. The show is an outlet for each participant's own validation issues. This particular desperation defines New York, at least in the song, the way Liza sings it. (Sinatra's version sounds cocky in comparison, missing the meaning and instead becoming a tourism ad.) It's drug addiction, abusive relationships, social climbing, sealing a wound, believing in a god that doesn't exist, living a romantic life hopelessly. My father, a real New Yorker, tells a story sometimes about working at a club where a young Liza sang at the piano. When someone yelled, "Sing 'My Melancholy Baby,'" she replied, "It's been done."

A definitive quality of this city is its constant transition (a contradiction). The cinematic images of New York that make it an attraction are dated, the places they depict stacked instead with tables displaying those very images, advertisements for the city once you're already in it. A cluster of distractions from the landscape behind them have become the landscape, iconic of the most commercial city in its search for newness. Times Square today is, as it ever was, boundless competition for attention, marquis posters and screens. In the newer version, we are advertised fantasy lifestyles, whereas decades ago the fantasies were more explicit, a striptease that called itself as much. Now, text builds like tattoos collected by someone who wants to forget their past by covering it up, words that become less resonant or sincere the more they are layered. Ads try to use white space to compete with noise, dusty color to compete with neon, block letters to compete with names in light.

Big cities are their navigation systems: public transportation, bridges to outer areas, highway traffic, barricaded streets for parades. They are not their stores, which could be anywhere. The way a city sees itself is sometimes by its most popular map, which is misleading about physical area because it stretches out the congested centers for easier viewing. It sometimes sees itself as its skyline, which changes because buildings and walls are erected or fall. It sometimes sees itself as a moment, perhaps the moment when a building or wall fell and the residents pondered the city and themselves, a collective definition formed by something drastic enough to hold their attention again. In paintings that depict time because they must, the skyline shifts. In Chinatown, a block is renamed Dimes Square after a restaurant that reminds me of California. Down the street, fake license plates and T-shirts being sold in kiosks say, in unison, Mafia, Trump, #1 Boss, Drunk Bitch, New York Fuckin' City, and Fuck You You Fuckin' Fuck.

Fire

Ever since the first day of the looting, a near-constant stream of fireworks has been erupting around my apartment and around the world every evening and into the night. Conspiracies are swirling. Everything these days is a distraction tactic. I suppose fireworks have always been that.

You would think companies would stop their third-party branding projects at a time like this, but in fact the design firms might be the most important teams to hold on to, image being so vital when everyone is mostly accessing things to buy via screens. In other words, brands must prioritize branding, not product, in precarity. Impressive amounts of time and money go into rethinking an image, just because the image might not seem capable of handling a situation. Now, it's more like two concentric situations: *pandemic* and *civil unrest*. Such soft little terms for such thorny, daunting issues. At work, we had to rebrand ourselves, too.

I walked to Times Square at the beginning of our quarantine to see it empty, but it wasn't quite. Photographers wearing surgical masks had staged professional cameras on tripods, trying to get that perfect shot of an abandoned metropolis, while ducking from the outstretched hands of beggars. I watched a guy who didn't appear to be on crack or homeless ask for directions and a photo-grapher telling him to "get the hell away," treating the whole place like a zombie playground, living his fantasy.

Amid ads for frozen vegetables and teen underwear brands telling us to go home, some opportunistic artists had tried to rebrand Times Square as a gallery, seeing as advertising space had become more affordable. These flashing works—calls-to-inaction in the form of pencil drawings—were not more beautiful than what is typically on the same screens and garbage can façades. Each of them coyly asked, What if fine art were here, instead? And of course, there is no difference.

I am one of those tourists in a not-empty Times Square, too. I'm trying to take in a lot of information about changing the world in easy ways. I don't trust anything totally. I hear ideas about hiring differently, dismantling a system, letting a system rot, letting the raw core show through. Branding doesn't protect you if what you need protection from is the brands. Or the cops. Or brands in bed with weapons producers, or whatever. My job is to make things seem different than what they are. And I want to do my job, because I'm good at it, and I want the money. I love brands like I love people. They did all start out as people, you know. Brands protect me when they pay me. I also want to do good, but I am skeptical of most do-gooder agendas. I want to sound like I care, but I don't want to sound like I think I'm not complicit.

"How do you live in a moral grey area?" my therapist asks. It might be helpful to imagine this moment as less nuanced than others. The fireworks going off might be some covert tactic that proves to those incensed by them that if cops were gone, chaos would reign. In truth, though, the police cannot protect the city from its own little explosions.

I went to a protest and one of the people on a megaphone ended up being identified as a counterinsurgent. So instead of working toward abolishing the police, I guess I was chanting along with some male model who was negotiating with them. Someone else, a person running for Congress, has turned some marches into their personal campaign rallies, it appears. Looking into their platforms before I voted, I noticed an endorsement from the Guardian Angels, a vintage vigilante group that roams the streets and subways wearing red sateen jackets and berets. Just a week earlier, I happened to meet a reporter covering the protests, who told me he had audio of the head Guardian Angel defending a McDonald's from looters. His first job was at McDonald's, he said, and he was "loyal to the golden arches."

New York is in phase two of reopening businesses, which means restaurants are going from takeout to sidewalk dining, and clothing stores are letting a few customers inside. On the news, I hear that the number of daily new coronavirus cases in the United States has not even peaked yet. Each phase of reopening makes the city feel more like Europe. We're drinking in public, eating on tiny tables outside, and, coincidentally, driving the new rideshare scooters. I walk through boarded-up retail neighborhoods to the occupied City Hall. Through mud, medics sprint from every direction when the crowd echoes an emergency. There is a long line for a gourmet buffet of donated meals. Staring at a man wearing an inflated Tyvek suit, I feel that there will always be too many people who try to make a moment about themselves.

Was Hitler even a good speaker? People always say that, but they say that about Trump, too, who mostly yells in circles. His latest speeches are about "defeating the radical Left, the Marxists, the anarchists, the agitators, the looters." He asks rhetorical questions and gets lost in tangents about Confederate flags, Antifa, Nazis, outer space, statues. But then every potential candidate running against him has a hard time speaking, too. Being a good speaker is, as far as I'm concerned, the one thing a president should be able to do.

Hundreds of thousands of people have left New York City, many of them to summer homes or Upstate rentals. My friends are buying cars and property. The white flight happening now started before the looting, though. It happened when the stores started closing, not when those same empty stores were broken into. Way before the pandemic, technology had been steadily changing the way people buy and find products, emptying retail and office spaces all over the world.

When residential neighborhoods cleared out like it was August in March, and everyone still here was forced to isolate in tiny apartments while showrooms and movie theaters mocked us with their emptiness viewable beyond thin panes of glass, our quasi quarantine pushed us into our screens even more than usual (and the usual was quite a lot, but I wonder if we will remember that, years from now). The advice that media outlets offered felt tone-deaf to our fatigue, listing streaming movies to watch after a day of streaming work, streaming the news, or staring at an unemployment form online. Our screens were our captors and our escapes. Uneasiness crept through our interactions. Going outside was viewed as irresponsible, but people had to be outside, especially if they were poor. Plus, it was starting to get nice out. Leisurely walks and boozy picnics were discouraged but allowed. So we tested the viral-loaded air. A man walking three German Shepherds pleaded with two police officers to shut down Tompkins Square Park, to arrest all these people out here, to stop the spread. The women in uniform sipped to-go margaritas.

Seeing the destruction in SoHo was like seeing a fire hydrant open on a hot summer day. Walking with my boyfriend one night, we turned a corner and witnessed an empty cop car burst into flames. People of all ages gathered around it, everyone exhilarated, before a team of firefighters dutifully put it out. Next, we saw a large group of policemen, apparently stranded, halt a tourist bus and direct the driver to charge full speed through an intersection. We saw kids having fun and taking photos. We saw stores getting broken into and abandoned, their products left on the floor. High-end gyms, super-branded clothing stores, and wellness merchandise shops had busted windows, whereas bookstores and smaller galleries did not. Pillows and slippers from store displays were strewn all over the cobblestone streets. Every bank in the neighborhood had been hit the hardest, their double-glass panes now mountains of shards.

The gesture of looting is symbolic, otherwise it would be called "robbing." That said, it literally opens doors for others who may or may not share an agenda with looters. Those who had the least to lose and the most to gain could simply walk in and take. It's about leveling a playing field. It's about ridding objects like monuments and money of their power. All of this, I recognized then and can easily recall now, looked legible in a sea of confusion and conspiracy. And to those of us exhausted by illegibility (campaigns to choke the media, protests that haven't agreed on a goal, the assumed bipartisanship of a virus) the sounds and sights in SoHo were bell-like, as welcome as a well-worded speech.

Social Suicide

I permanently deleted all my social media accounts and then I told the people I ran into, not realizing it might have the same grating effect as a newly sober person bragging to a lush.

"We're still in prison," said Jean.

"Were you having mental health issues?" asked Sara.

Deleting the apps felt like diving off a cliff into a deep, calm lake. There wasn't really a reason to do it other than the temptation to jump. I'm still addicted to looking. I'm also a defender of social media's artistic merits. Lately, though, I'm wistful for circumstances that gave me the option to flee into the relative unknown, abandoning a set of routines and expectations for something less predictable. When I was a merch girl for a couple of bands during college and just after, I didn't have a smartphone (I was a holdout) and can remember the feeling I had looking out the windows for hours, enthralled by road trip tropes like that stretching sensation brought on by rolling nothingness in all directions and the farcical qualities of rundown motels. I grew up with parents who worked backstage and was happy to be there again. I loved watching a show from a booth, alone while surrounded by people. I suppose it's all very millennial of me, but restrictions on socializing have me missing another time, even if what I'm missing is the absence of a thing, not necessarily the time of its absence. Maybe I'm not even missing that, and what I'm nostalgic for is any time other than right now. I wanted to feel like I was on a plane with no Wi-Fi, like I was being lifted into the sky.

"I'll give you three weeks," said Eve. "I'll bet you a dinner at Via Carota."

"You can always come back if you need to," said Kate.

Whenever I was contacted via Instagram about getting paid to promote products, I agonized over what to do. It would be a bad look, I thought, but then again maybe the irony of an author who dreamed up fictional influencers before influencer marketing was a thing becoming a shill for some rich person's vanity project would have an edge, I reasoned. Mostly it was the problem of turning down money. Either way, nothing ever came of those offers, and so after convincing myself to do something unsavory, I had to deal with rejection, too.

The one reason to be on any networking app is to get attention. Attention can lead to friends, sex, and money, but the attention itself is a thing, too. Dating apps are full of people who never plan to meet up with you but will devote hours of time texting with strangers. The more attention one gets, the easier it is to get it, and the harder it is to be satisfied with it. This isn't simply because of the addiction model, wherein we chase the original high with diminishing returns; it's because wider reach involves targeting the lowest common denominator. Selfies sell, etc. Pornography is deliberately unartistic. Effective advertising isn't overly intellectual. My interesting friends appear stupid and self-involved online, and that leads me to wonder: Do I? And: Do I care? I probably should, since, if we each have a personal brand, mine was constructed to sell books, get bylines, and appear hirable by cultural institutions.

"I quit Twitter and Instagram ... in the same manner I leave parties: abruptly, silently, and much later than would have been healthy," begins the *Bookforum* review of *The Twittering Machine*. A week or so off, I commiserated with Allie, who had been off a month. We were surrounded by friends taking pictures of one another with one purpose, looking out at the darkening river instead of our phones. Did you know that if you disable Instagram and then reopen your account, you're not allowed to disable it again for a week?

Allie is back on the app and didn't tell me, afraid I would shame her. Kate gave me her passwords, telling me to keep her off for two weeks, no matter how much she persisted. She jokes about what I will do with the access to her accounts; I try to imagine the equivalent to an addict accidentally overdosing after a sobriety stint, not being aware of her changed tolerance levels. I remember talking to a friend who is in AA about what people talk about there. She explained that everyone has a relationship to alcohol, and that most people don't think very hard about that fact. If they did, they would most likely see something scary. Your personality is all you have, really. It isn't fun finding out that yours is addictive, and that what you are addicted to invariably and irreversibly changes your behavioral patterns. It is, however, exhilarating to learn a type of self-control, I suppose. This friend is great at staying sober, but admits she's addicted to other things, like video games, and, of course, social media.

"He was inspired by you," Kate told me of her boyfriend, who got off social media, too. He was back within weeks, and it looks like he's posting more than ever: aggressive, pro–free speech thoughts, as if he had been told to shut up. My absence, apparently, failed to last as an inspiration, that being the nature of absence, as opposed to presence. There is no Social Media Addicts Anonymous, I don't think.

Another friend, one who never liked AA, started drinking after ten years of sobriety a few years ago. "What happened?" I asked. "I decided that I like life more when I'm drinking," he said. We got drunk together that day and it was maybe the most fun I'd ever had with him. To my knowledge, he's not on social media. I remember he tried Twitter a few times and couldn't get the hang of it. It was strange to watch, and a reminder that fantastic and charming people often flounder in these online outlets. Remember when we thought one-liners and dance routines were embarrassing? The thing is that no matter what, we're still on social media. I've had this suspicion for some time, arguing, back when it was an argument to be had, that Facebook was not just another thing on the internet, like Wikipedia or virtual aquariums. I'd get annoyed with people when they feigned disinterest in the idea, saying they hardly participated in the new tools of self-promotion. "I'm on it but I never post" sounds guilty, and at the same time naïve. Is a dependency on voyeurism healthier than one on exhibitionism?

When I quit Instagram, my time on Twitter ballooned. When I quit Twitter, I started a newsletter. Even if I quit that, too, I cannot escape; I know this. Attention-incentivized creativity is a presence in the atmosphere, never to be combed out. Like microplastics sloughing off the cheap fabrics we wear, it is around us, in us, on us, and being advertised to us, forever.

Kate cracks after five days. First, she asks me for the new password I assigned, and when I say no, she emails Instagram and they issue her another one, logging me out. I had been looking at it, anonymously, and then my access to the site was once again limited. I can see a preview version of the app, essentially. I run into yet another friend on the street who tells me he quit Instagram, too. "It was empty calories," he says. A surplus of time and privacy lent to unhealthy habits and bad posture. Anyway, much of the aspirational content that drives hate-follows and deep-dives has subsided due to the lockdowns. Everyone looks pathetic and poorly lit. It was past time to leave the party.

"My brain is broken," texts a friend who consistently deletes his apps and then reuploads them. "Sorry I haven't logged on, my meds are working," tweets someone who repeatedly mentions taking

Twitter breaks, too. "I'm retiring Twitter for three months on a trial basis" someone tweets on December 31, mapping out where else to find him in the interim: Instagram and a weekly open Zoom call. After several more tweets, he tweets the next day about how it will be his last for three months. He tweets four more times that day, and every day since, including a link to the Zoom meeting as it is happening. This is not judgment so much as it is recognition, I think. Or it's proof. Also, it's an anecdote to illustrate my lack of distance. I can still see all this stuff, obviously. "tfw you build societies off of dopamine-driven feedback loops," someone writes, on January 6, on the dopamine-driven feedback loop that is Twitter. Two days later, the remark had been liked 4.3K times. I was glad to not have the option of participation in such loops that day, the day of the electoral college vote protests. I could still hear immediate reactions, see memes, parse unformed opinions, have conversations, and get information concerning the event, although not necessarily in that order.

And then a bunch of platforms—businesses—banned Donald Trump, who is himself a business, and people cried censorship. I once wrote about an artist who had been cancelled, before that word meant what it does, as in all her upcoming shows and lectures were cancelled, due to a controversy. She was quick to say it was not censorship, though, since the establishments in question were not the public square. Museums have donors to impress, and they can do this by keeping a relatively low profile, keeping an outer circle blissfully ignorant of what makes art political. The artist's controversial project took place on Twitter, actually. She tweeted every line of a book that was taught in schools, and some of them, when singled out and left available for new contexts, looked racist. The controversy was that although she intended this work to be revealing of what does and doesn't get redacted from a record, some viewers only read the offensive lines individually, as tweets coming from an artist. The cancellations of her appearances caused a much bigger stir than the piece ever did, and so instead of getting art world audiences in person, she got a new following on Twitter, giving the project another set of legs. I'm not sure when the project was taken offline, if it was because the artist deleted it or Twitter did, but it and the artist's personal account have been suspended. After all, startups have investors to impress.

"This is why I left social media," I keep saying, every day, about something else. The plot is altogether unsustainable, I insist to anyone who will listen. At some point, if it seems like the red pill is being offered on the blue pill manufacturer's site, the least you can do is try buying street drugs instead. Still, I can't imagine being truly free, dropped into an Oz-like world without the incentives of gamified attention or humiliation monetization. The outside appears exotic, with flowers as bright and shiny as Technicolor plastic that somehow isn't shedding microfibers into our lungs and bloodstreams. Or maybe it's more like returning home to a soothing, sepia-toned Kansas, wide open and targeted ad–free.

"I'm taking a break," say so many of us, maybe announcing an upcoming project right before we log out, trying to keep some ambient attention directed at us as we fall off the map. The message about leaving disappears as our accounts do, and so when others go looking for us, to find nothing, they might assume something—a nosy boss, an uptight significant other, online suspension, strangers piling on in the comments, a new private account, suicide. Or they (a collective they, not any one person, whom we could simply ask) might assume we have gained a new outlook on life, one that doesn't involve constantly updating a public, the goals of these updates becoming manipulated over time until it is us, not them, who are to blame.

"You should totally play *Cyberpunk 2077*," my friend Chris tells me. The ads for it, which I've seen on bus stops and billboards around a boarded-up Manhattan, are in the same headspace as his paintings, uncanny collages of modern emblems and cyberpunk tropes, in which computer desktops take on an acid neo-noir color scheme, collapsing soon-to-be-dated graphics and past renditions of a fictional future. His newer works are made digitally and printed in layers of acrylic, ink, gesso, and UV resin, giving a rugged, earthy texture to elements typically found on screens. Magenta, cyan, green, and fluorescent white are created using a combination of underpainting and image transfer, a technique that helps them glow like pixels. Digital lines fuzz, as if seen through watery eyes.

"Have you been feeling dissociated lately, like this has all happened before, but in a movie?" I ask him over the phone. All we see on the news are makeshift hospital tents, autonomous zones, abandoned centers of culture and commerce, and surveillance vigilantes holding flags for cult ideologies. The déjà vu comes from recognizing narratives that inform today's scenery.

In the genre of cyberpunk, which Bruce Bethke christened in a 1983 short story (though its origins can be traced to the 1960s), broken communities and ecological catastrophe act as counterexamples to the dreamscapes of other science fictions. Cyberpunk worlds also tend to take place in a more extreme version of the present, rather than a wildly speculative distant future. Here, the media manipulates viewers' bodies (*Videodrome*), humans are made into cyborgs (*RoboCop*) and vice-versa (*Blade Runner*), corporations and governments plant false memories into gamified brains (*Total Recall, eXistenZ*). As technology advances, the genre argues, the average quality of life deteriorates. Cybernetic body horror serves as metaphor for an increasing fuzziness between lived experience and corporate agenda.

On a podcast, one woman comes up with an ad hoc business plan for the other: monetized newsletters, panel cameos, TV writing jobs, essay collections, editorial positions. She could *easily* make a lot of money, which is the beauty of being a creative today, they agree. I add emphasis because even if these jobs might be *easier* than others, they are not easier than what they used to be. They only make sense in combination, and they are never-ending, all-consuming: work is life is work, and your reward for doing a good job is more work. Writers (photographers, sex workers, vintage dealers, talk show hosts) join subscription-based content-seeding platforms, offering anything people want from them, a next-level selling out. The shift has been called the "hustle economy," a more frenzied version of the gig economy, a model that famously moved money away from cab drivers and hotels with ride- and home-share apps, only to dangerously accelerate gentrification and raise the cost of living.

Cyberpunk 2077 (an iteration of a tabletop RPG launched in 1988 and set in 2013) is narrated by Keanu Reeves, who happens to bridge many cyberpunk spheres by starring in all four *Matrix* films and the 1995 film adaptation of William Gibson's *Johnny Mnemonic*, which is set in the "Second decade of the 21st Century. Corporations rule. The world is threatened by a new plague." After almost a decade of false starts, *Cyberpunk 2077* was finally released in December of 2020, only to be pulled seven days later by Sony, due to customer complaints—just another glitch in a year that already felt *Matrix*-like. In other words, gamers hoping to enter a virtual landscape (during an actual government-issued quarantine) were largely unsatisfied that the game didn't accurately depict a made-up post-apocalypse due to unsettling bugs.

Chris lists the similarities between our present and those depicted in some of his favorite movies, books, and games: "24/7 shopping, a world being ravaged by the spread of a fast-moving disease, twentieth-century postwar alliances falling apart, an impending climate catastrophe, a reality-show president, James Bond villain—like strong men running rogue states, increasing distrust of authority at the civilian level, surveillance mechanisms at a scale the likes of which has never been seen in our history, untold concentrations of wealth and power lying with the very few, growing racial discord, alarming and repetitive state-sponsored hacking, politics as entertainment …"

He invites me to his timeshare in the Hudson Valley. A pure white newborn baby cow frolics in the fenced-in field adjoining ours as we make lunches of farmstand produce. At night, the Milky Way is visible beyond silhouettes of foliage as lit up with lightning bugs as Christmas trees. Walking a pitch-black path, we spot a massive comet suspended in the sky and hear a pack of yelping coyotes. The next day, a hidden kid next door serenades us with Tourette's-triggered screams. A short drive takes us to a "poet's walk" and to a "swimming hole" dotted with smooth rocks that perfectly seat small groups of White Claw–drinking friends. The landscapes that roll by from a car window caress that part of my brain desperate for loudly green stillness. Before I can open a book to read, I look up and the day is almost over, nothing accomplished other than getting ready for it. This is the Upstate feeling, the feeling of no wasted time, there being no time to waste. People always talk about wanting to get away and do nothing, but in the rural enclaves where they go, the chores are never done.

In the hustle economy, everyone becomes their own product, and this tramples an already sputtering underground, luring even the most subterranean of content creators to its neoliberal landscape. The contrarian, the politically incorrect, and the avant-garde are celebrated, platformed for all they're worth. A subculture doesn't have to be small, just underexposed, and what counts as exposure, now, comes semi-organically, mostly from anonymous rubberneckers. Network television, magazine covers, and even billboards seem so quaint as benchmarks, their carefully controlled deals so archaic, so elite as to be niche. These are the people we admit we know the names of, but have never seen in action, while, under pseudonyms, we interact obsessively with the celebrities that won't get movie roles. But there's far more money in livestreams.

At one point, to be involved in a subculture meant defying expectations by refusing to participate in some youth-hungry industry, such as sponsored skateboarding. Once we all stepped into the pinball game of the social network, though, selling out became an obsolete concept. Our definitions of subcultural groups began to rely on the businesses to which they subscribed and the monetary systems in which they traded. These platforms and currencies are articles of style, what amphetamines were to the mods, ska to the rude boys, and bondage wear to the punks, to use the prototypes from Dick Hebdige's *Subculture: The Meaning of Style* (1979). He wrote, "The meaning of subculture is always in dispute, and style is the area in which the opposing definitions clash with most dramatic force."

"I feel like the future is fully here," Chris emails me, echoing the circa 1993 William Gibson quote, "The future is already here, it's just not very evenly distributed." In 2014, Gibson said that his stories were never meant to predict the future, but to "get a handle on the present, the present having become extremely fantastic."

The World

The original date for Akeem's show was postponed due to the pandemic, delayed an entire season until phase four of reopening. A sign of unpredictable times, the purportedly last ever China Chalet party, thrown in March of 2020, was announced as a celebration of this show. Then, with no event attached, the gathering was instead an oblivious send off to the restaurant itself.

Akeem was at that China Chalet party that was no longer for him, which surprised me. I was seated near him at a wedding, once, and during the family speeches, I overheard him plotting an escape for another event. He waited out the three-course meal like a student in detention, polite but perturbed by how uncharacteristically overdetermined his evening was. At China Chalet, the coming curfews were part of an unknown future, and so a precarious, even chaotic energy was palpable. Traipsing in and out of the second-story club, the ex–guest of honor was in his element.

Actually, Akeem said, he was relieved to have some extra time to finalize his debut. The audience for this body of work was not just the art world or the fashion world, but his family and mentors, namely the subjects of the pieces being shown. More so than any of his previous endeavors, the roll-out had to be perfect. And as the photographers and fashion designers with whom he regularly works will tell you, all of Akeem's projects are not really confirmed until they're finished. Presentations of his clothing line, for example, are notoriously mysterious in terms of date, location, and city. If the work isn't right for the moment, it simply doesn't happen.

Growing up between Kingston, Jamaica, and Brooklyn, Akeem was raised around the dancehall design collective Ouch. He's been working on "the archive" of their ephemera and footage since he was a teen. Now, it was installed among articulated materials like painted wood and breeze blocks shipped to Manhattan from Kingston. The scenery recreates and distorts the content's previous contexts and the sensation of being outside looking in via the liminal settings of partially outdoor nightclubs.

"There's a weird nocturnal economy within dancehall," Akeem explains. "For instance, Mister Morris would take your photo, and at the next party, you would buy it from him. This was his bread and butter. He wasn't a photographer that wanted to sell prints, it was more so, I'm gonna take a photo of you and you're almost guaranteed to buy it." Now, of course, things are different. Everyone with a smartphone is their own Mister Morris. In another example recounted to Akeem, cameras at Kingston parties were at times only there for effect. "Apparently, they'd think having a video camera livens the party. Now, it seems intrusive, but before—and this was not even that long ago—it was about the video light. At the end of the party, the guy took the roll and broke it. He only wanted to video the party so it would be hype. That was their psychology."

At the show, behind curlicue fences and layers of corrugated metal, people from another era peek and pose. Closeups of hands pulling at panties look even more salacious laid flat on the ground. The viewer of any archive is in some ways a voyeur, and we are made to feel acutely so within these installations, climbing through bedroom-like walls insulated with old sheets. Scrap-wood barriers are collaged with fliers, flags, and graffiti that state "Don't touch," or the Jamaican maxim "Remember this: When you come here, what you see here, what you do here, what you hear here, when you leave here, let it stay here, or don't come back here."

"It really isn't even for our generation or anything in the present," Akeem tells me. "It's for the people in 2120, 2130, to have some sort of historical context. People are already gonna look back at some of the films and say, Oh my god, I can't believe people behaved that way with a camera. But this show is for even later generations. I always used to wonder, Shit, what used to happen in those sugar shacks in Alabama?"

Maneuvering around body-like shapes bulging out of vinyl corsets and a massive custom speaker system made to mirror those carted out for the block parties of Akeem's adolescence, I sense that the show was once meant to be more shrouded in its own presentation, camouflaged by crowds of fashionable people. But the opening is constrained by pandemic-era health measures, and only a few people are allowed to see the art at a time, leaving the reconstituted dancehall memories slightly eerie. It is as if we are already in some distant future.

On my way home, I pass a building that in the 1980s used to be the home of a club called the World, where, apparently, a lot of firsts happened, such as Björk performing in the United States. When we read about the '80s and its parties, there is always mention of an epidemic, the AIDS crisis, and how it set a tone, acting both as deterrent and impetus for going out. Partiers showed bravery, or maybe it was nihilism in the face of certain oblivion, the end of the world, for which this former club was named. People liked to party like it was their last day on earth, like it was 1999, like their lives were in danger, and they were. A good party requires a sense of urgency, heightened by secrecy, and during recent years, it's been hard to keep anything a secret. Even if parties are illegal or exclusive, they are surveilled by their own guests. Guests whose lives are mostly online develop competitive natures, and soon every exciting event can't not be broadcast to their followers. This structure leads to sponsorship, obviously (the opportunity for organic reach is irresistible to brands). And so, in the 2010s, the underground nightlife scene gained a moneyed polish. Bars were set with glowing, labeled glasses, and people stopped doing things they wouldn't want to be photographed doing. Each era has its pros and cons. We had free, themed cocktails at least.

But in 2020, the shame associated with partying, in relation to the coronavirus, got rid of the sponsors, for better and worse. The party hosts are living on unemployment, without a lot of options, but then again, there is potential for that urgency and escapism we always hear about to return. I used to wonder, If underground parties go completely corporate, what will future generations think of us? It depends on what the future is like in comparison, I guess.

There were always exceptions. The Spectrum, a queer club in Brooklyn, did everything it could to stay underground despite its popularity. It was always threatening to shut down because it wasn't legal and needed extra funds to pay off violations, I assume. Located at first in a sweaty house in a residential neighborhood, with a bouncer standing on a small, gated lawn, it moved around, its name becoming synonymous with a crowd more than a space. When friends tell me about missing the Spectrum, they talk about a sense of intimacy that they have not been able to find anywhere else.

There was, we can appreciate now, a unique uncanniness to the phony layers of those sponsored parties, though. I remember working an event at the now-closed Pacha New York, the massive space on West Forty-Sixth—near Larry Flynt's Hustler Club—infamous for its policy of not giving back change if one paid for drinks with cash. This party I'm recalling was real, but it was also staged, as it was being filmed for a Nile Rodgers & Chic music video. We were, by default, extras. The strangeness of being watched while partying was inhibiting but also exhilarating. The multiple takes of a supermodel getting out of a cab in freezing weather didn't even make it into the video, but we got to be there for it, watching from inside. That's the tension we're chasing at parties, after all—it amounts to otherwise impossible inversions of status, however momentary.

When a space is shut down, it becomes legend, the meeting spot for a cross section of a time. I often think about Passion Lounge, a Bushwick club with a mirrored staircase leading up to a balcony, before it got renovated and renamed Republic, and later closed. For a short moment, it felt like everything emergent in New York was being performed there. Then, the dim sign with its silly backward *S* became this oppressive LED marquee, and I stopped hearing about anyone going. China Chalet was like a cockroach, always coming back when you thought it was dead. It was filled with smoke far after the ban and the tables were streaked with cocaine, but during the day it was a functioning restaurant. In retrospectives, it is being called "our Studio 54," even though no one called it that a year ago. And it is that, if only because the idea of this location will stand in for a scene.

"There's a piece called *Social Cohesiveness*," Akeem told me before his opening, smiling at the title's accidental echoing of the phrase of the year, *social distance*. "People are doing things together but unaware of what they're building. There're certain social cues that we don't recognize now because we're living them."

Above and Below

A man who fell into a sinkhole in Queens says the sidewalk crumbled under his feet; it felt like a suction was pulling him down. He free-fell for some time and then landed in a swarm of rats. People on solid ground above asked him to yell out to confirm he was okay, but he did not open his mouth, for fear that the rats would go inside. (Still, everyone hates LA. They're coming back to New York, as soon as winter is over, they tell us.) Also this month, a man in China was arrested for causing a traffic jam by throwing money out of his window, possibly while high on meth. It was described by local media as "a heavenly rain of banknotes from the sky." The sinkhole in Queens was described as "another sign of the impending apocalypse" and "like a portal to hell opening up." My first week in New York, I met a woman whose friend had just fallen through some rusted-out sidewalk cellar doors. "It makes you think," said the woman. "There's a whole world beneath us." Today, a senator said, "Who the hell elected you?" to a multibillionaire tech CEO testifying in court. The senator was angry at a type of information flow that is biased by the money that can be made from attention. The product is defined by consumer interest, like most things. We all got checks signed by the president, when all the stores were closed. So much money is being printed, and there is so little to do with it, now. Sometimes, it flutters down from the sky like the autumn leaves, and we are reminded that there's a whole world above us, too.

"What if you don't believe in God?" asked James.

Dierdre kicked him under the table. One woman, Dierdre's aunt, smiled at the question. It was more like a smirk.

"No really, what if you don't believe," he tried again, looking around the table for eye contact with anyone. Dierdre's head was bowed but her eyes were tilted toward the ceiling. She was cutting a piece of chicken with a steak knife. "It's hard to draw the line, then," he added. Again, no one responded.

Dierdre's aunt gave another sad grin. It was condescending this time. "If something helps humanity," she started, and then trailed off, "I mean, well." She put a forkful of coleslaw in her mouth.

"Humanity," Dierdre's cousin scoffed from across the table. "Humanity would best help itself by dying off, don't you think?" He looked younger than everyone except for James and Dierdre, maybe in his mid-twenties. He had been easily distracted throughout the dinner, sometimes getting up and looking at a photo on the mantle. It was as if he, too, had never been here.

"People used to say that so much was 'playing God,'" continued James. "Abortions, robotics, sex changes. But then you have orthodontics and prosthetics and—I mean, is internal medicine playing God? Is hypnosis? Is air travel?"

"Yes but," Dierdre's father interrupted, "why are we even talking about this." The way in which he said it was meant to end the conversation. It did. The chicken was tough to saw through, with tendons fraying until they snapped and pockets of cartilage setting knives off their paths, causing the awkward sounds of metal skidding across ceramic. James could feel his own heart beating, and so he sensed Dierdre's father's heart, a new transplant, beating, too. Mr. King was not supposed to drink alcohol or eat red meat after the operation, Dierdre had told James, which explained the inexpertly prepared meal. They were all used to something else. A glass of scotch, neat, hardly left Mr. King's hand that evening, though. With each sip, James pictured the heart—a pig's that had been decellularized until it was pigmentless and for this reason sometimes called a *ghost heart*—evaporating. The alcohol dripping directly onto it, burning like acid. Liquid soaking into each ventricle, drowning some whirring motor until it sputtered out.

The procedure was expensive, dangerous, and so new it was considered experimental. Mr. King had suffered through a long recovery time, during which Dierdre had spent many weekends visiting home instead of going to her first college parties with James. The pig's heart had been put through a mysterious scientific process to empty it of the qualities that make it pig-like, Dierdre had said, using words that didn't seem right but which she swore the doctor had used, like "detergent," "matrix," and "scaffolding." They can do this with plants, now, too. They can make a graft out of something that is neither human nor animal, she had said, her eyes bloodshot.

Mr. King clutched his drink. As if his hand were hiding the glass instead of bringing attention to it. Mrs. King's face didn't show signs of a frown, though. The thickness of her expressions, the offset wrinkles that were maybe less pronounced but likely more noticeable because of their misplacement—pleats pointing at the bridge of the nose instead of whiskering around the eyes, broad folds above the top lip parenthesizing the nostrils—managed to mask judgment. She was one of those women who had surpassed appearing any certain age. James wondered if, for her at least, this was the desired outcome. She didn't dress youthfully, although he had to guess that at some point she had, maybe when she was young, maybe sometime after that. She could have been trying to turn back time, to preserve it, to slow it, or to split the difference, but ended up with a compromise that simply looked unnatural, if only slightly, which is all it takes. If she had waited a few more years, the cosmetic surgery field would have advanced enough to avoid all this. They can do things with plants, now. The years can be erased from the skin, now. The absence of time, grafted on. James had seen photos of decellularized spinach leaves. He had seen vascular plants taking in nutrients through cut stems and wet roots, food coloring rising through the veins of a celery stalk, vines climbing windows with centipede-like feet. James could swear he saw tiny scabs where Mrs. King's forehead had been injected. The more he looked at it, the more her face looked like shaved foam.

"What are you majoring in?" she asked James. "Do you know yet?"

"I was leaning toward economics."

"That's a good field," said Dierdre's aunt.

"Yes, but I'm getting more interested in philosophy."

Dierdre looked up from her plate at him. Her aunt audibly sighed.

Beads of sweat collected on the sides of his glass, a stemmed, cylindrical glass containing what Mrs. King had called a "dry rosé." When he visited his mother, James didn't have a drink at dinner. He wasn't of legal drinking age, and even though no one was trying to keep any secrets, laws were abided, if only out of habit. After his twenty-first birthday, there would be some remark about letting him grab a beer before joining the adults in the family on the porch, he was sure, but there would also be some performative shrugging, some show of it all being a show. This is what you get, for waiting, for pretending to wait, at least. This is the substance rewarded to people that have aged: an ice-cold one, a dry rosé, a glass that looks so tightly gripped it might burst, tearing the fine skin that holds all these tissues in place until they decay from the inside out. The peeling silver scales on chapped fish flesh. Oyster mucous on white-lipped shells that grow in mud. Root vegetables drained of color and peeled of hair.

Dierdre had seemed ecstatic on the bus ride to her hometown, saying that she knew her parents would like James. She'd placed her forearms on each of his shoulders and clasped her hands behind his neck, the way she always did. She'd pointed out features of the town from the window as they approached the station, where her mother was waiting in a car. She'd leaned over the front seat to talk to him on the twenty-minute drive to the house. How were the dogs? She'd asked her mother. A pain since she was the only one who took care of them anymore. James adored dogs and would love to take some for a walk, Dierdre said. We'll see, said her mother. James loved Dierdre's enthusiasm for incidental things like dog walks and bus rides. She'd gradually gotten quieter as the conversation dulled, though, and as they dropped off their bags in a bedroom with that once-lived-in look that brings some mothers to tears, Dierdre's energy plummeted. At dinner, her eyes were glazed, her small hands focused on the utensils and meat in front of her.

She had the same wide-set face of her mother, nothing of her father, a close resemblance to her cousin, who was talking, now, about his decision to go back to school for a degree in gender studies, eliciting mixed responses from all the adults. She was the first girlfriend of his who wanted to introduce him to her parents, the people who created her. They would continue to create her, even as she was creating herself, even after they were dead, and she was stuck remembering her childhood and spending their money, if they had any. Her features would become like theirs had become, until a certain point, when she would get a new face, a new heart, or discover what these lives would look like without them.

The top button of her father's flannel was unbuttoned. The shirt strained around his belly. Every so often, he would remind the table that he was listening to their conversation by saying "That's nice," in earnest, or "Real nice," sarcastically.

The pig's heart was no longer a ghost. It had attached itself to Mr. King's insides and sprung to life anew. It had prolonged a life and become the clock by which the family told time, and yet it was not born into the family, was not even born into the species. The metaphors conjured by the words *pig* and *heart* were inescapable and yet unutterable. Dierdre, James knew, would not appreciate him questioning her father's insatiable passion, the hunger for life that one would need to go on living, he thought. The glass of scotch was emptied. The family finished their meal and began clearing their own dishes. The night trickled along, as if it was not blaringly strange and sutured.

A friend of a friend has a new facial modification, some kind of glowing implant to make it look like a neon circuit board is beneath her skin. Also, she has a fake gash down her forehead: permanent prosthetics and tattooed color that mimic an always-open human wound. The wound, importantly, does not reveal metal or wires. The body mods encompass two diametrically opposed ideas occurring in one space, on one head. She is not simply *cyborg*—a cybernetic organism that is built from both living creature and robotic parts—but *simultaneously* animal and android, bleeding and bloodless. She (in photos) appears oblivious to the paradox I see. For this look, contradiction is inconsequential. The statement, whether intended or not, is about draining images and language of any fixed meaning.

Lauren says she goes to the library and reads old issues of *Seventeen*. We have always had the same problems, she reports, which means we have not solved them with the advice offered by magazines. If beauty is in the eye of the beholder, the beholder's eye is another algorithm, imprinted with rules that later determine what it sees. In an alternate history devoid of popular culture, without the tracks of mass media to follow, human eyes could have continued to individualize, forever. *Beauty* would carry a meaning more like *satisfaction* or *struggle*, words more often associated with the personal than the universal. The diversification of beauty standards is being pushed by people onto corporations, but also by corporations onto people. One hopes to be seen as beautiful and the other hopes to be able to project beauty ideals to a diversified consumer base. If everyone gets what they want, no one does. McDonald's is a sponsor of body-positivity panels and sporting events.

I can't find the high-speed pop song "Gonna Have Fun," performed by a group called Sirens, anywhere other than the movies *Ghost World* and *Storytelling* (both 2001). I assume it was produced for film, sarcastically, as an invented example of mainstream music's emptiness—the antithesis of authenticity (a theme of each movie). The song itself has stuck with me, though. Its clipped pacing is a lot like some double-speed TikTok tracks of today. Plus, in each suburban context, the lyrics ("Gonna have fun, in the sun, 'cuz you're the one, we're gonna have fun") are meant to sound unbearably shallow and so are imbued with the depth of bleakness. The characters complain about popular music throughout, stating at one point that a band is "so bad, it's almost good" and that it's "so bad it's gone past good and back to bad again." In *Wilson*, another movie based on a book by Daniel Clowes (author of *Ghost World*), a car radio plays Carly Rae Jepsen's "Call Me Maybe," to protesting groans from a similarly cynical set of characters. The song is just as saccharine as "Gonna Have Fun," but now the complaint feels more earnest because it is about a real-life pop hit, and something is lost.

"I'm not usually this bitch," I say to a friend, "but she dresses horribly. That, or I just don't understand it." I was confident, though, that I did understand this horrible outfit. A few days later, I saw a different girl wearing the same outfit components, exactly as I'd described them, and she looked incredible. Either she had pulled off the look better or I had become obsessed with my own initial reaction, transforming disgust into desire. This is the meaning of fashion, to me.

There's a billboard near the Manhattan Bridge Arch showing a very square handbag edged with Gucci-esque bamboo and the words, "Barney's said our brand had 'no direction,'" which makes me cringe because *Barneys* is not spelled with an apostrophe. And then on closer inspection, it makes me cringe again because in this image, there is nothing obviously disproving Barneys's point. The implied narrative, I guess, is that the fittest brand (between a century-old department store and a five-year-old bag line that went viral last year for a tote printed with the words "End Systemic Racism") survived. Still, the ad lacks the frisson it was after. Besides the typo, the contradiction it presents isn't adequately illustrated because a square is the most directionless of shapes.

For her wedding, my friend designed lighters that say the names of the couple and the word "forever," which is maybe a clever way of saying, Whatever *forever* means. Lighters do take forever to empty, but not literally. And then, nothing is literally forever, least of all the classic wedding favors: bubbles, rice, bouquets, tea candles from table settings, etched champagne flutes. I keep hearing about fentanyl in cocaine like it's salmonella in spinach at the grocery store. Don't buy right now. Wait out the infection. But also, there are drugs everywhere, in restaurants and parks and cars. The relentless optimism of everyone feels threatening.

We're buying a lot of nothing now, but shopping for its own sake isn't new; retail therapy, a concept as old as me, implies that psychologically, we are not really after items, but purchases. Still, businesses must compete for customers, even if what customers are buying is the chance to buy. Because we're in the era of redefining shopping, we're in an era of redefining life. The calibrations we see now favor schemes to sell more nothing, to give us nothing—an escape to nowhere, a video of a box being opened, a certificate of digital ownership, a TV show consisting of people watching TV.

I sometimes inadvertently imagine a physical version of the content created by content creators, one of those massive file rooms from conspiracy films. Hot paper is being spit out of old printers. Someone comes in and picks up a scrap to read, can't figure out where the thread starts, becomes a raving lunatic and has to be carried out on a stretcher. Instead, we get to have nothing, which is, if you think about it, the most futuristic part of life today.

We ourselves are nothing if we're not something. A TikTok star I'm watching on TV is worried that his numbers are going down. He clings to the schemes on which he once relied to grow engagement: controversy, romantic posturing, cross-pollination, a sped-up, saccharine disposition. One get-rich-quick scam has so far succeeded, but as the teen ages out of his own target demographic, a quicker plummet proves itself a possibility. A new strategy is needed. And so he joins the cast of a reality show. Here, he pivots to what does well on TV: a fleshed out, slowed down backstory, interpersonal drama, tears at a gravesite. All of this, every single thing that is happening on these screens, is done to make money.

But advertising is not nothing, it's one of the most substantive acts we have. I am reminded of the monologue from *American Psycho* that goes, "I have all the characteristics of a human being: blood, flesh, skin, hair; but not a single, clear, identifiable emotion, except for greed and disgust." I search for it, noticing that another popular search is for the skincare products Patrick Bateman uses during this scene. Those are not real products; he is a character in a movie. None of this is real. Incidentally, I have a cooling gel eye mask like his. When I bought it, I was probably attracted to it because I had seen it before, on him.

Retrospective

Art Club 2000's most resonant work today is a series of photographs included in its first show, *Commingle* (1993), in which members of the collective pose in what could easily be mistaken for ads, wearing identical Gap outfits. Twenty years later, in 2013, founding members Daniel McDonald and Patterson Beckwith told *Artforum*, "We chose the Gap because it represented nothing: a gap." Now, it represents more than that, or rather, the art world has read more into it, in part because of *Commingle*. Influenced by the show, which made a satirical comparison between empty consumerism and art school, collectives such as DIS and K-Hole emerged, working as artists, but also as consultants for hire.

In 1996, Art Club made a replica of Kenny Scharf's Scharf Shack at the American Fine Arts entrance for their show *SoHo So Long*. The windows of the gallery were soaped out and decaled to look like a transitioning Old Navy storefront. (For the 2020 retrospective, the same treatment was applied to the windows of Artists Space.) These pieces acknowledged the blurring lines between art and commerce, but also of an evolving New York: instead of a new Gap taking over a SoHo gallery, a pop-up store offering merch such as a Scharf-faced Swatch had appeared, its painted entrance either grinning or clenching its teeth, depending on how you looked at it. Art Club's inclusion of the shack in their survey of SoHo pointed to the hall of mirrors downtown had become, with mall brands and underground artists merging into retail galleries.

When DIS was asked to curate Red Bull Arts' inaugural New York show in 2014, they created *DISown*: part gift shop, part gallery, part radio station, part open bar. The exhibition in effect transformed the energy drink–sponsored art space—which happened to be in an old Barneys Warehouse building—back into a department store, with commercial products on display, such as salad bowls, body pillows, and toilet paper created by contemporary artists. The same year, K-Hole coined the term *normcore* in a free pdf report called *Youth Mode*, part of their semiserious trend forecasting practice. Studying the paradox of blending in as creative expression, the normcore chapter was not meant to describe a way of dress but rather a mode of being. The term, however, resonated with fashion writers who were, at the time, faced with a sea of overtly bland outfits worn by the types of people who once defined a fringe identity, namely artists. *Normcore* became synonymous with a certain style that reappropriated inconspicuous, low-end basics brands, such as Uniqlo, Crocs, and, of course, the Gap. In tandem, DIS, K-Hole, and similarly structured collectives became increasingly influential in the art world, offering branding work to clients both corporate and avant-garde, at once measuring the sustainability of commercial collaboration and testing the limits of art propaganda.

Before Art Club 2000 came the Offices of Fend, Fitzgibbon, Holzer, Nadin, Prince, and Winters (formed in 1979). The Offices was not a collective, they insisted, but a consultancy. They put out ads in art magazines and carried business cards that looked like those of a law firm. In fact, quite a few artists formed marketing agencies in the 1980s, especially those whose work mimicked or iterated on the era's prevalent advertising methods. Louise Lawler and Sherrie Levine had a publicity firm called A Picture Is No Substitute for Anything. It's difficult now to see the artworks of these collectives as separate from their side hustles: consulting for non-art entities, feeding the beast that eats away at art practices, infiltrating the spaces from which these artists drew their ideas would eventually become part of the project—self-appropriation, backward validation.

The Offices offered "practical esthetic services adaptable to client situation." If the group had ever gotten hired for anything, I guess they would have had to see what compromising with a client looked like. The consultancy was founded on the principle that making art in the non-art world felt more viable at the time, in terms of financial stability and audience, since the art world was too hierarchical, its reach too insular. But then, the '80s was a time of commercials taking cues from art, post peak Warhol. It was a time when the role of artist was thrown against a wall and dared to reject the power and currency that the market could potentially provide.

In the late '80s and '90s, Gap ads had started to feature niche luminaries of the art world, in a campaign called "Gap: Individuals of Style." There were photos of Joan Didion with her daughter Quintana Roo, composer Ryuichi Sakamoto, architect Maya Lin, and gallerist Leo Castelli, in dramatic black and white. To promote *Commingle*, Art Club 2000 provided *Artforum* with a parody ad featuring its gallerist Colin de Land. The Gap threatened to sue, but, judging by an even-toned letter from their lawyer—which was on display in a vitrine at the Artists Space retrospective—corporate wasn't too worried. Maybe some Gap executives were even excited, after so doggedly courting the art world, that real, young artists had noticed.

Further conflating the mediums of artwork and ad space, *Gap: Individuals of Style* showed at the Museum of Contemporary

Photography in 1994, only a year after Art Club's *Commingle* was up. Another museum show, *Individuals: 20 Portraits from the Gap Collection*, showed at the National Portrait Gallery in 2007, and included images of Jim Dine, William Burroughs, and Dominick Dunne. In most of *Individuals of Style*, artists wear the clichéd black turtleneck, uniform of the avant-garde. Didion even did this twice, once in 1989 for the Gap and again in 2015 for a Céline ad.

The Gap's '90s strategy was predicated on celebrating the rich inner lives of bland dressers. Another campaign used vintage photos of stars who "wore khakis" during their downtime—movie stars, but also artists such as Warhol, Ernest Hemingway, Salvador Dalí, Miles Davis, and Arthur Miller. These images are from a time before the Gap existed, overlaid with text that tells its audience about a lifestyle to buy in to, bigger than a wardrobe to buy. Cynically, and successfully, the Gap became a branding experiment, providing emptiness for shoppers to "fall into." It asked whether clothing even mattered, or if what a customer really wanted was the thrill of consuming, cushioned by the promise of conformity. It stood for nothing, as Art Club 2000 members recounted in 2013; it represented an actual gap, the space between the things that beg for attention or rigor. By 2014, nonfashion was fashionable again for artists, perhaps nostalgic for a time when stores didn't regurgitate every trend moments after inception, overwhelming the market with instantly accessible diversity. The Gap of the '90s, or that void of branding it once stood for, looked like a reprieve from the demands of high and fast fashion.

The intertwining of art practice, management studio, and publicity machine continues. The semiotic square that introduced the term *normcore* sold as an NFT for 3.5 Ether, meaning, loosely, that the concept of normcore has been bought. And yet there is a "multiplayer networking plugin for Unity" called Normcore, made by a VR platform called Normal, and the word itself has been subsumed by a fashion ideology, translated by Michael Kors to *NormKors*, which to me looks more like the opposite corner of the square, *acting basic*, defined as "being returned to your boring suburban roots, being turned back into a pumpkin, exposed as unexceptional," while normcore is "all about adaptability, not exclusivity." In other words, there could never be a normcore style, in the original sense: it is, by definition, the absence of conviction.

Part III

Conspiracy

"I knock on this door, and I go in and it's a nice suite. There's a young woman there, half undressed; she has a trench coat, which she's just taken off—there was money in the inside pockets of the trench coat—she has an open briefcase on the bed with money in it, she's taking money out of her brassiere." So says production designer Robert Boyle on *Who Killed 'Winter Kills'?*, a documentary short that accompanies a DVD reissue of *Winter Kills*, a comedic fictionalized exploration of the assassination of John F. Kennedy. Boyle isn't describing a scene from the feature. This exchange, he says, happened behind the scenes. "That's how I got paid."

"And then," says director William Richert, "we found out somebody shot and killed [executive producer] Lenny Goldberg—somebody he owed money to. They blew his brains out. They handcuffed him to his bed." Not mentioned in the documentary: another executive producer, Robert Sterling, was sentenced to forty years without parole for narcotics distribution and other charges.

Winter Kills (which Boyle has called the "most delightful" film he's worked on) bobs and weaves around the unsolved murder of an American president named Kegan, pausing to focus on the interpersonal relationships that make conspiracies so difficult to predict or trace. It's one of six films curated and introduced live by artist and conspiracy connoisseur Jim Shaw at Metrograph. The program includes two of Hollywood's best depictions of justified paranoia set in earth's market-driven, alien-run future, *They Live* and *Total Recall*, as well as some deeper cuts.

In *Investigation of a Citizen above Suspicion* and *Leo the Last*, a protagonist is painfully aware of his position within a corrupt, cushioned inner corridor, in the former as a murderous police chief, in the latter as an heir to a dethroned royal family. Each can't help but be curious about just how far the networks that protect them stretch. The spoiled but suspicious heir in *Winter Kills* follows clues that lead to ever more nefarious discoveries about his powerful relatives. In one horrifying aside, President Kegan's father mentions that he is undergoing blood-replacement therapy: "I take it from the kids at Amherst. Got a deal with the Red Cross."

Jim Shaw has been thinking a lot about the proliferation of conspiracy theories in the past couple of years. He'll watch any documentary about one, no matter how unprofessional, he tells me before we enter the theater to watch *So Dark the Night*. If copyright law didn't matter, he adds, he would have chosen some YouTube rabbit-hole discoveries for his series. "For me, and for anybody that's entranced by conspiracy movies, by true-crime podcasts, by endless depressing documentary series about horrible events that took place at some boys' school sometime in the '70s, it's stimulating the frazzledrip in our brains."

Frazzledrip was, as far as I can tell, invented by people at the website NewsPunch (formerly YourNewsWire). According to some threads on Twitter, the term comes from the filename for Anthony Weiner's personal footage of Huma Abedin and Hillary Clinton terrorizing a child before drinking her blood in a satanic ritual. This term, one surmises, is slang for the release of adrenochrome, an excuse for torturing a virgin sacrifice these days: in a widely shared theory, panic causes the chemical compound to be released into the youth's blood, which consequently becomes the perfect elixir for evil energy harvesters.

Conspiracy, or the dramatization of it, conjures another kind of energy. "There's an aspect of conspiracy theory, and everything that engages people with, say, QAnon, that creates a sort of adrenochrome in your brain by stimulating it," Jim says. "It's like frazzledrip is a frazzledrip. The idea of frazzledrip gets someone who believes in frazzledrip all excited in the same way that torturing children is supposed to bring about adrenochrome … That's kind of what goes on in the cinema." Soon, the lights dim, and the next movie rolls, opening with a sex scene that turns into a bloody murder.

Adrenochrome, by the way, is a real thing, and scientists have been interested in its properties for decades, without publishing much in the way of findings. Its name has been dropped in literature and song lyrics since the 1950s, mythologizing it into a rarefied drug found only in living humans. *The Doors of Perception*, *A Clockwork Orange*, and *Fear and Loathing in Las Vegas* all describe adrenochrome as a psychedelic. Rich people filling their veins with fresh blood to stay young, like the joke in *Winter Kills*, is real, too. According to a *Los Angeles Times* article from 2019 ("As age-obsessed billionaires turn to 'vampire' therapies, the FDA takes a stand"), the government recently issued a warning against the injection of young donors' plasma. Older patients would pay $8,000 a liter, said one start-up that offered the injections.

However, science-backed institutions have found no evidence that young blood, whether full of fear-induced chemicals or not, is energizing, mind altering, or age fighting. Still, many conspiracy theories posit that institutions have much to gain from spreading false information about such things. Either way, the news being reported from all sides is that there are in fact American sex cults entrapping young people to pacify the elite. And when, say, Jeffrey Epstein's life and death are at least as sinister as any vampire fiction, the defining characteristics of a reliable narrator start to blur.

When Jim Shaw was installing his three-story takeover of the New Museum in 2015, he found that he was missing a video component for *The Hidden World*, his massive collection of propaganda from "secret societies, evangelical and fundamentalist movements, new-age spiritualists, Scientologists, Freemasons, ultraconservatives, and all kids of conspirators." So, he tells me in an email, "I looked for stuff on YouTube and found endless docs about the Masons, pedophile conspiracies, etc. Most had an English-accented narrator that I realized was a computer voice reading a script to give it 'authority.'" This started yet another content collection: a list of conspiracy-themed movies, from film noir to "the various low-budget documentaries that helped me through [2020] and stimulated my dopamine receptors … usually featuring a narrator droning on about the Illuminati with cheap panning graphics."

Jim's work tends to face far outward, seeking and hoarding alternative forms of truth and religion that would normally never enter New York art-world circles. In his collages and collections of media and marketing, messages contradict one another using similar languages, in turn muddying their individual initial intents. But in these wandering, decades-long surveys of fringe thinking, he is looking inward, too.

Born in Midland, Michigan, Jim graduated from the University of Michigan before getting an MFA from the California Institute of the Arts. Just out of school, he got a job doing sketches of "the dream of a god and prehistoric animals made from living ones" for Terrence Malick's planned follow-up to *Days of Heaven*. (The project was put on hold and only released several decades later as *The Tree of Life*.) Other film and advertising jobs included "designing monsters for a Corman *Alien* rip-off called *Forbidden World*, a couple of months airbrushing on *Tron*, a four-year stint at [Robert Abel and Associates] working on high-end FX commercials, various stints at DreamWorks doing the effects animation for *A Nightmare on Elm Street 4*, and a scene in *The Abyss*; I designed the titles and alien fur and spaceships for *Earth Girls Are Easy*, then there was a 3D CGI thrill ride for a Sanrio amusement park …"

A Midwestern sensibility and a fascination with the theatrical are plainly felt in Jim's sprawling yet somehow humble art, which comes in the forms of scenic painting, video, installation, and other mediums. And his extensive experience of the mechanisms that animate so many runaway imaginations has not inured him to their effects. In fact, ever since he's been behind the scenes in the production of thrillers, simulations, arcade games, commercials, and cartoons, he's only grown more fascinated with the extended lives of certain science-fiction and horror scenes as they appear in countless paranoid hypotheses, especially since, as he says at the screening of *Investigation of a Citizen above Suspicion*, "conspiracy theories exist because conspiracies do."

Meaning power-hungry people who want to live forever *do* pull society's strings; that these strings are so intertwined with everyday life means that they are indecipherable. Movies that metaphorize conspiracies such as the ones in Jim's list stimulate in the same way a YouTube explainer does, frazzledripping down our washed brains as we attempt to determine truth from trope. Fleshed out with bouncy Ennio Morricone soundtracks, sexy actresses, and Franz Kafka quotes, these movies simplify complex themes in the style of the truth-revealing sunglasses in *They Live*. We see the curtain and what stands behind it, all while getting wrapped up in the excitement of falling down a rabbit hole. Then, leaving the theater, we might wonder, If that was all okayed by studios, commercial markets, and investors, how much of the story wasn't?

As cynical as *Winter Kills* seems, for example, the making of the film was apparently as dark and tangled as its script, inadvertently proving some greater point about what happens when one attempts to reveal something seedy using the same systems behind such seediness. The story goes that the shoot was shut down multiple times because the crew were not getting paid by the production company, which had only ever made softcore Italian sexploitation before and had hired a first-time director based on the recommendation of their first pick Miloš Forman's agent. After the death of Lenny Goldberg, Richert came up with a plan to finance the half-done bankrupt film: he took its stars Jeff Bridges and Belinda Bauer to Germany and directed another movie with them, *The American Success Company*, which raised enough funds to get *Winter Kills* running again. To recap, a movie set in Germany about an American credit card company ("AmSucCo") saved a movie made with dirty money about the American government's endless plots to keep its citizens ignorant. And then *Winter Kills* (budget $6.5 million) bombed, making just over a million at the box office. But maybe that was because it was blacklisted for unpatriotic sentiments.

The movie was based on a book, and the book's author, Richard Condon (who worked for decades in Hollywood before becoming a satirical novelist), later wrote a piece for *Harper's* about life imitating art. There he described, in as much detail as he knew, the whole crazy tale of *Winter Kills*, including its inspiration. In 1963, after the American public learned that many groups and individuals had motives for murdering JFK, Condon writes, "Overnight, a belief in conspiracy came to be equated with raging paranoia. To believe in any conspiracy against the government was paranoid, the public was told again and again." Richert told Condon that, when reading the book, he'd thought it "too far-fetched, too criminal, seditious, incendiary, poisonous in its rendering of the big time," but that "since making the picture I've met all the types."

When the star-studded film was finally released, it won ecstatic reviews but was pulled from theaters early and never widely distributed. Everyone had their own theory about why. "It was 1979," writes Condon in 1983. "A presidential election was coming up. Avco, which was the parent company of Avco Embassy [distributor of *Winter Kills*], had revenues of $864,646,000 that year for its products and services, and these included important contracts with the US Departments of Labor, State, and Defense. It is tempting to speculate that Avco might have felt it expedient to please powerful political friends"—meaning the Kennedys, in particular Ted, who was campaigning for the US presidency—by killing *Winter Kills*.

Jim tells me to read the story of the making of this movie as itself a twisted conspiracy theory about the Kennedys and the American government at large: there's the controversial murder, the conspiracy surrounding it, the narratives spun out of hypothesizing, the suppression of such narratives, the stories of suppression, etc. So goes the endless stream of theorizing uploads online, which often use popular cinema to explain themselves, even when said theories claim that Hollywood is an evil agency.

Making connections, no matter how far-fetched, is intoxicating. We are taught to search for meaning in narrativization, and so we do, constantly scanning for revelation. Also on Jim's recommendation, I watch homemade video after homemade video, their slapdash, train-of-thought structures part of their allure. Some of these adrenochrome explainers, for example, are exciting to watch because through them we can witness adolescents trying to untangle their own mindsets from social conditioning. As I am inundated with wild theorizing in every direction, it all starts to blend, becoming a bigger story about what people do with guilt.

Investigation of a Citizen above Suspicion centers on a detective who commits murder but is naturally not considered a suspect. Knowing what he does about his department, he is intentionally sloppy about hiding clues when he commits the crime. His prints will soon be all over the scene anyway once he is called in to investigate. Eventually, he admits to himself that he has waffled between wanting to get away with the crime, to prove the existence of absolute authority, and wanting to be caught. He breaks down, believing that everyone exercising power over citizens, such as the police and politicians, internalizes this dichotomy, and that they cling to a kind of sadomasochism. His addiction to danger produces diminishing returns, so he resorts to killing a woman and later torturing a man, getting a thrill from the suffering of others at his hands—suffering for its own sake.

In QAnon thinking, the suffering of the innocent has a purpose, and the greater the suffering, the more innocent the sufferer, the greater the outcome for the offender. I ask Jim what he thinks of the obsession with tortured kids that binds so many alternative worldviews together. Based on a few examples of acquaintances, friends, and famous people, he hypothesizes that "if your emotions are severely stunted, you might need the slaughter of the innocents just in order to get any emotion. Abortion horror has been a unifying issue for the conservative Christian Right for five decades, and I think the whole Illuminati baby-blood-drinking thing just goes along with that mindset, as well as the need to think of one's enemies as the most horrifying entities imaginable. The fact that there are several organized groups like the Catholic Church, the Boy Scouts, smaller cabals like Jeffrey Epstein's or Cyril Smith and his pals, that allow, overlook, or use pedophilia for influence, makes fantasy conspiracies like QAnon seem possible. And being out of work or holed up (or both) because of COVID for long periods of time, and plenty of time to kill on the internet while algorithms feed you the most alarming information? It's a perfect storm."

The Cult

"Can I read to you some lines from a play my friend wrote? It's really great, she's a great writer," said some guy in the courtyard, who probably didn't even see me there. This guy was talking to someone else, someone who wasn't paying attention.

"I'd like to hear it," I said, "under the condition that you perform it. Maybe let one of us read a part."

The guy didn't turn to face me or look over his shoulder. "I'm not doing that," he said.

"Stand up, at least," I said.

"No."

"Okay," I relented.

He started to read from a phone screen, turning slightly to signal a shift between two roles. "Have you ever wondered why all the lines on a street are painted either white or yellow?" Turn. "I guess I haven't, no." Turn. "You never have?" Turn. "I have not, but now I'm curious." Turn. "I looked it up, because I wanted to know." Turn. "And?" Turn. "I don't know. I still don't know."

I looked at the other guy, to see his reaction. He was looking at his own phone.

"I still don't know," repeated the first guy. "I love that."

"Wait," said the second guy. "Can you start over?"

I went back inside the building and down the hall to the apartment, to the party. The friend I'd come with dutifully met with me to report. "That guy over there was in a cult."

"Which one?"

"A new one. Like, he *joined* a cult, wasn't raised in one."

I stared at the guy, in a peeling pleather jacket, now walking quickly toward and past me. He stopped somewhere behind me and started talking animatedly to someone else. He said something about Tucson, Arizona.

"Did you say Tucson?" I interjected. "I'm from there."

He nodded and then kept talking to his friend. It was time for me to leave, I thought.

"Wait." The cult guy blinked at me. "You're from Tucson?" The information had taken a moment to register with him. "I lived in Flowing Wells for nine months."

Everyone knows the popular reactions to the mention of their own hometown. I was used to hearing about a visit to a retirement community, a spa, or a trade show.

"Flowing Wells?"

"Yeah." His eyes were sunken, his mouth dry.

Another guy approached us. "Wow, hey," he said. "Do you remember the last time we saw each other? That was so insane."

I wandered away again. There were no glasses left, so someone had brought out a plastic-sleeved stack of small blue cups. The sleeve looked greasy. I filled a cup with room-temperature vodka and cold soda. Pleather Jacket was behind me again.

"Sorry about that," he said. "I wanted to talk about Tucson."

"Sure." I was starting to get bored already, imagining the dead end of this topic. Hometown talk is like weather talk, and it usually includes weather talk, attractions that locals never visit, wildlife that no one really sees. Still, I asked, "What did you do there?"

"I was a sign spinner," he said, "through a service that, like, hired sign spinners."

(135)

"You were a sign spinner in Flowing Wells, Tucson?" I glanced at the people around us, but surely no one else would be able to understand this statement's depth. "I worked at the mall near there."

He smiled, looking relaxed for the first time.

"What made you move there?"

"A friend of a friend let me stay with him after I was kicked out of a cult that I was in. I had nothing because I was in a cult. Tucson was the closest place where I even kind of knew someone."

"A cult." I feigned surprise, but also, I was surprised he brought it up.

"I was in a cult, yeah." He leaned on a wall for balance.

I didn't have to ask him to keep talking because he wanted to. He didn't look around him at all, just at me and at the floor.

"They described themselves as a cult at first. They don't anymore, but they still are. They're still going, only with a few people, but, yeah."

"And you escaped?"

"Yeah."

"Why?"

"The human trafficking."

"Okay." My temples throbbed. "Do you smoke?"

"No, but I'll come outside with you."

We were the only two people in the courtyard. He explained that he was in recovery therapy, that he was working with a lawyer, that the cult started with a couple that took him in as a student. In a way, he was a founding member, having rounded them out to three. The aims of this nascent organization sounded idealistic. They wanted to dismantle systemic bigotry and create art for the modern world. They needed help with recruitment and fundraising. The cult grew, at first as a sort of music school, then as a way of life.

The founders and members moved all over the country, living in relatives' homes and shithole motels. Members were not allowed to work within the American capitalist system but were expected to pay dues. Eventually, everyone was in debt to their leaders.

Somehow, I believed every word he said. His voice rattled faintly and not unpleasantly, like a ball in a spray paint can. I listened to descriptions of Facebook groups, meme styles, pseudonym generating methods. When I looked it up later, I found only one article and some posts about the Day Life Army, so named because the founders rejected a nightlife scene, I gathered. In the article, this guy told a reporter the same things he told me, that members had to become not only recruiters but prostitutes and beggars, since selling one's body or the ideas of the group were the only Day Life–sanctioned transactions. Members were instructed to masturbate while watching types of porn by which they weren't typically aroused. They ingested their own and one of the leaders' semen. They had homosexual intercourse if they self-identified as heterosexual, with the goal of ego death. The article didn't say it, but it seemed obvious that these practices, aside from being power plays, were designed to make more versatile hookers. Everyone was stripped of their resources. Their time was spent on social media spamming their friends, families, and outer circles. Days and nights that became years were spent jerking off, posting PayPal links, and catfishing strangers on dating apps—a scene from a movie that has yet to be made about a particular time in history.

Someone else entered the courtyard. "Is he telling you about the cult?"

I was disarmed by this new stranger's buoyancy. He must not have known about the human trafficking. I nodded.

"Dude. Wild, right? But there were things about it I get. Right? Like, we need something that does what they were trying to do."

"What do you mean?" I asked.

"I mean," he sipped his cigarette, and I sensed a rising impatience with me already. I was suddenly aware I was older than everyone I'd spoken to here. "Someone has to transform these things we do online only into a physical, livable reality, to replace this totally outdated, retarded—as in *ritardando*, so don't even— *system*, this total bullshit art world." He flashed air quotes, making the cigarette nod.

"He's an early influencer," said the cult guy, as an introduction. "Maybe you've seen him."

"No," I said. "I mean, have I?"

"I was, like, the first person to do Instagram."

"To do Instagram?"

"To do, like, fashion, there."

"I want to know more about the cult," I said. Even the simple description of it somehow deepened my deepest fears. These leaders had exploited an obsession with rewriting culture, walking people right into the most obvious of brainwashing tactics, such as replacing vowels in words to sever past associations they might conjure. If the earth is flat, maybe everything is. Money, meat, and all that is in between can be replaced. Events can be forged. Memories can be lost because we learn new ways of describing ourselves all the time. The project of human life might never be put back on track because the experiment was a failure. If there are accidental cults, then anyone can be in one, unknowingly.

"What do you want to know?"

"Did you like Tucson?" It was a terrible question.

"Not really."

"Are you going to stay in New York?"

"If I can work it out. I'm trying to get back into music." He started describing a new project and I started to space out. Eventually, he walked into another conversation. He had not asked me anything about myself, a relief.

I left the party with my friend and told her about the conversation. "He was a sign spinner in this neighborhood that's, like, nothing."

"So, no one could see his sign?"

"No, it's busy there, but it feels like nothing."

"Is he still brainwashed?"

"Probably. There's no way he's not."

"How does he have any money now?"

"I didn't ask."

"There are no sign spinners in New York."

We walked up Seventh Avenue past a halal cart that smelled of hot oil and a fusion restaurant called Taco Mahal that was closed. I was hungry, and because I was thinking about Tucson, I remembered the twenty-four-hour restaurants there. Not diners, more like parking lots with order windows. They made burritos for each time of day and had salsa bars. Someone on Christopher Street was leaving a deli carrying what looked like a Caesar salad in a plastic bubble in a plastic bag. We walked for a while longer before splitting off in the different directions of our apartments.

The latest posts by the Day Life Army announced that it was ending. I had been told not to believe those. Images were covered in intentionally misspelled, humorless text. Posts from ex-members decried their time in Day Life. But whether a post was asking potential cult members to deny an oppressive system or asking current cult followers to deny the methods with which this group oppressed its members, it took the same negging tone.

At one of my old jobs, I received daily mass emails from a guy who claimed certain colleagues of mine had physically and mentally tortured him for years. These were long and incoherent, with dozens of slightly altered versions of the same mirror selfie, a picture of a muscular shirtless man. They said that my coworkers and employers were part of an exploitative sex cult with ties to government organizations, detailing stories about sinister meetings that he'd witnessed. These people he named all knew him well but had black-listed him after he wouldn't participate in their crimes, he insisted. I asked around, and others in the office were getting the same messages. No one recognized the author.

"Just a psychotic gay," one colleague said, annoyed by the emails but not as alarmed by their content as I thought he'd be. It said that this colleague in particular was a masochist and a cuck who would never squeal because he loved the torture too much. Once, I responded individually to a thread, simply asking its sender to stop contacting me. My work inbox was full, and I had to keep deleting old messages to even receive mail at all. In the next mass email, the sender had added me to a list of the complicit, copying my private message to him as evidence I intended to silence him.

Sometimes, something in these emails would catch my eye. Words such as "exegesis" or "pseudosatire" seemed worth a deeper dive. But the volume alone was enough to make the story impossible to follow, and I had no choice but to block the multiple addresses from which its chapters were sent. When I got a new job and a new email account, he didn't contact it.

I visited Tucson, but my favorite tourist attractions, the ones that had been emptying for decades, had been obliterated by the travel bans, it appeared, and yet the slow gentrification of downtown near the campus had rushed ahead, pushing businesses off the main drag but hardly filling in the gaps left, causing a confused reshuffling that made me even more of a stranger in my own city. I looked for a favorite Mexican spot, an old candy store, a kitschy Japanese restaurant, and a friend's vintage shop, but each had moved just a few blocks away into charmless spaces, forcing me to reevaluate their products. The cool, spiraled layouts and glazed-tile bars, tatami rooms, or chipping murals had been what made the experience, I was forced to see.

"The Golden Nugget is all cleaned up," my nephew smiled. "And it's just called the Nugget now." We were holding sweating beer cans in the back yard of my ex-sister-in-law's house. I'd only ever gone to the Golden Nugget because I'd once lived near it, in an area that felt out of range for college kids at the time. Apparently, it, like the surrounding grocery stores and restaurants, had recently been revamped to attract incoming students.

A system of pierced hoses draped around an awning made with corrugated plastic let off a pleasant mist that soaked the dogs lying on the outside rugs underneath. "We might go to the bar later," said my older brother, holding out a glass pipe and lighter.

"You mean the Nugget?" I asked, wagging my hand at the weed.

"The bar, the game bar," he corrected.

"It's called A Short Rest," said another nephew, the youngest. "And yes, I happen to be a dungeon master there about five days a week."

A short rest is a dice roll in Dungeons & Dragons, which even I know, although I've never played. The game's philosophy was as close to religion as we got growing up. Life is a series of dice rolls, a chain is only as strong as its weakest link, what he lacks in brawn is made up for in brains, etc. When I was a kid, the gaming happened at my oldest brother's place, a little house with two Dobermans named after Greek gods. Only the men in my family played. I was not invited to A Short Rest, unsurprisingly. It's inside the mall, my dungeon master nephew told me. "And, yes, it's open later than all the stores, and so they had to hire a special security guard so that people don't accidentally exit the wrong way and get locked in."

"I might head there now, if someone wants to give me a ride," said my dad, maybe wanting to get this part of the day over with. The guys got in their cars and drove off, continuing one of the several D&D campaigns in which they were each involved. The game doesn't really end. There isn't a winner, anyway. The characters were brought up in everyday conversation as if they were real, as if their actions, decided by six-sided die and the dungeon master's whims, were as interesting as any human's. I felt the fear of parallel universes creep over me again, the fear that I had missed some valuable lesson about life by never double-living as a semifictional avatar. I knew that there were people who entered fantasy realms with the intention of gaining life skills and there were those who went in intending to escape life, but that these people were really the same.

I had a friend pick me up. "Have you heard of the Day Life Army?" I asked. We were in her car, driving toward Gates Pass to catch a sunset. I tried to explain the premise, but since it wasn't about Tucson, I could feel my audience losing interest. This was a story about the weirdos one meets in New York, how interesting *my* life had gotten, or about how cults still exist, which of course they do. "This one makes people think it's all a joke, part of this long, drawn-out meme, which is how they get you, I think. It's, like, a cult for the extremely online and yet they are spending all this time going out to the middle of nowhere."

"A lot of people in the super rural areas are extremely online."

"I guess that makes sense."

"Did you hear about Amadeus?"

"Amadeus. Was he that guy that was at every party, just ignoring how much older he was than any of us?"

"He's a *lot* older than us." We were silent for a moment, each of us making some calculations. Were we closer in age now to our memory of Amadeus, or to our younger selves? "I think people felt safe around him."

"What happened?" I asked.

"Is that always how these things go?"

"What did he do?"

"I don't really know. A bunch of guys accused him of things. Coercion. He promised people things, apparently. It's all in some letter, signed by a bunch of people, and I've never seen it. But he left town. Moved away and blocked everyone. He must be in Mexico. Or maybe he moved back to where he's from."

"He's not from here?"

We had parked in the little lot designated for the lookout point but stayed in the car. The view was fine from where we were. The sun turned into an egg yolk slipping through the mountain peaks, its shape changing from orb to blast. The cloudless sky around it was not turning pink or purple. Still, a crowd of people perched on the rocks ahead of us was audibly impressed. From what I remembered, Amadeus had not so much promised people things as much as he had suggested access to another world. Opportunities to enter elite spaces without putting in the work of social climbing or getting hired. He knew fashion models and photographers, he said. I vaguely remembered that he took some boys on trips to bigger cities, where they were cast as extras in commercials or hired to bartend events in tuxedos. Amadeus didn't appear to have a lot of money, but he did have rich friends. To us, at the time, he was an example of what one could do with nothing, seeming one way and living another.

The sun disappeared and it was dusk. We drove to an old bar neither of us had entered in years. It was open, but almost empty, lit with heat lamps from tropical pet tanks. We drank fishbowls until we were screaming.

The next day, the Tanque Verde Swap Meet was the emptiest I'd ever seen it. The Dragon Wagon was abandoned in front of a dried-up bumper boat tank and a corral of faded rental strollers, but somehow the koi pond was still lively. My ex-sister-in-law found a booth that sold fabrics she liked. They could be layered onto the costumes she wore at the Society for Creative Anachronism, where members LARP multiple pre-seventeenth century eras at once, she intoned. One of my nephews was interested in some old manga character figurines. I was day-drunk and only halfway through a twenty-four-ounce crab-red michelada, squinting behind sunglasses at a cloud of dust kicked up off the ground, wanting nothing, really.

We were near the airport bar and a lot of other empty parking lots: gravel, dirt, concrete, tar, brush; flat tones in blurred concentric stretches up until the sage-purple mountain ranges with their jagged outlines. The mountains that were just as colorless as anything else when you drove up to them. A familiar feeling returned from when I used to live here, some simplification of desire. This place, the desert, was clearly the other side, where people are disposed. I remembered walking aimlessly, the edges and metal rivets of my jean jacket getting hot to the touch, when my emotions weren't drained but dried out, or drowned in cheap beer. On our way out, we got lost in a spiral of highway exits. On one desolate corner I spotted a sign spinner for a car wash. He was wearing wraparound sunglasses and baggy pants, which should tell me something about what kind of person he is, I thought, but really, he could be anyone: a cult member, a dungeon master, a car wash owner. If this was a movie, it would be when I discovered an answer to the question of why the lines on the roads were painted white or yellow. But that was never a question, to me. It's because the roads, before fading to grey, start out black.

The ex–Day Life Army member posted a photo, a group of people including himself. He wrote about reconnecting with the friends that had also left their cult, and concluded that in some ways, it was all worth it. To give oneself up so completely to a cause and then find one's way out was, if traumatic, also life-affirming. In the end, he wrote, he had learned a lot.

The Director

"This is a cursed corner," says John, as we walk past the burned-out Middle Collegiate Church on East Seventh Street and Second Avenue. A fire destroyed most of it in 2020; another fire, five years earlier, made four apartment buildings across the street unlivable, killing two. We look up at the remnants and back down to Second Avenue, our gazes falling upon a couple. The dark-haired woman is likely in her early twenties and the white-haired man simply looks old. They pass us.

"Girlfriend?" John guesses.

"Probably," says Daniel. "That was Abel Ferrara."

As movie theaters reopen, each decides if programming moves ahead as previously scheduled, or if priorities should be reconfigured. For its return, Cinema Village ran a retrospective of Ferrara's work. His newest film, *Siberia*, didn't get an in-person premiere, a good enough excuse as any to celebrate his legacy now. I wonder, though, if there was something more to the decision to forefront this oeuvre, and not that of some other indie director who made a straight-to-VOD movie last year.

Ferrara is not twee nor even PC, but he's also what some might call uncancelable, a label saved for artists whose subjects are problematic yet treated lovingly, who always escape accusations of exploitation or romanticization due to some vulnerable interplay between creator and character. Ferrara has made a cult career of interrogating the uneven tempers, power hunger, and resulting shame of characters who share many traits with the filmmaker. These men are usually around Ferrara's age at the time he writes them. They are alcoholics, Bronx-born, filmmakers, sober, Buddhists, living in the East Village, living in Rome, taking Italian proficiency classes, married to a woman played by Ferrara's real wife or ex-wife, the father of a kid played by Ferrara's real child, or working on an upcoming project that shares the name and themes of Ferrara's next film. By putting his own untoward desires and behaviors under a microscope, he can analyze his movie's motives before a reviewer can. As one wrote for *Slant*, "What saves it from presumptuousness and superiority is the readiness with which it admits its ignorance."

Still, the films playing at Cinema Village—*The Driller Killer* (1979), *Ms .45* (1981), *4:44 Last Day on Earth* (2011), *Pasolini* (2014), *The Projectionist* (2019), and *Tommaso* (2019)—noticeably skip over the '90s, by far my favorite Ferrara era. The later films mostly see the mild-mannered Willem Dafoe as muse and stand-in, whereas for an entire decade, Ferrara's protagonists were largely played by a creepier Christopher Walken—*King of New York* (1990), *The Addiction* (1995), *The Funeral* (1996)—or a rougher Harvey Keitel—*Bad Lieutenant* (1992), *Dangerous Game* (1993). I can't help but think that, with this omission, either the programming staff at the theater or the filmmaker himself are playing it a little safe.

Take the most unsparing portrait of his frustration with Hollywood and with himself for courting it, *Dangerous Game*. Here, a fictional director, Eddie (Keitel) pushes his lead actress, Sarah (Madonna) by breaking down her confidence. The character Sarah is difficult to extricate from the person Madonna, one of the most conspicuous people in the world, in 1993 and now. And so when Eddie calls Sarah a "commercial piece of shit" from behind the camera while she tries to recite her lines, we feel for each of them.

Then, a sex scene proves too real for Sarah and a new level in the metafilm emerges. Sarah/Madonna looks at Eddie/Ferrara and cries, begging him to stop the scene. Her distress is more than convincing, especially, I assume, for an early-'90s audience, only familiar so far with Madonna's music career and her handful of PG roles.

Upon its release, Madonna expressed disinterest in promoting *Dangerous Game*. Ferrara, incensed, chalked up this decision as premature embarrassment for what she must have assumed would be a flop, like her previous Hollywood forays. On the contrary, *Dangerous Game* was applauded for its uncompromised look at the snowballing effect of an auteur's control. And in a way, Madonna's departure from the movie's press cycle acts like a coda, revealing Ferrara's real-life insensitivity toward his hitmaker. And for this, Ferrara may well have been what we call "canceled" today, the meaning of which we have yet to figure out.

What are the canceled artists doing these days? John Galliano, the head of Maison Margiela, has returned to making lighthearted videos for *Vogue*. Tao Lin's new book is getting rave reviews. Louis C.K. has sold out Madison Square Garden again. Some artists have lost followers but gained new audiences. We can all agree, can't we, that each case should be judged individually? We will attempt, as objective viewers, to separate the artist from the work, but in truth, we will not be able to. And if we're being really honest, we'd like to know how it felt, especially if the artist in question was, previous to the accusations, making work that concerned power dynamics. A comeback, in these cases, should continue to interrogate authority and its abuses, with gained perspective.

C.K.'s comedic work, for example, tended to explore guilt, desire, untenable expectations, humbled situations, and the reality of American dreaming. A joke from his 2020 stand-up series

Sincerely Louis C.K. (the first since he was fired from so many projects in 2017) mentions that he never could have prepared for the feeling of knowing that everyone, "even Obama," is aware of his sexual fetishes. Here, his discomfort is on display, if in his control. He is famous, he reminds us, and we're relieved by this, since famous people are less deserving of privacy. We, the audience, want C.K. to suffer a little. We know how he got here, and that however far he fell, his landing was cushioned by a pile of money. It occurs to us that it might be better for the psyches of the abusers, the people they hurt, and everyone learning of the abuse if past behaviors were not revisited. In the moment, though, we agree that exploring the leadup to a scandal will more likely benefit us. We want to know: What makes a person behave in a way that will humiliate others, and eventually themselves? How does a pumped ego amplify or suppress certain voices in one's head? Powerful people in media have a responsibility to behave professionally. But would they have had the confidence to behave so unprofessionally, had they not achieved such power?

"Can Louis C.K. Spin His Troubles into Art?" asks Hilton Als's February 2020 *New Yorker* review. "Couldn't he go there, Richard Pryor style, and talk from the vantage point of his disgraced penis? Instead, he let his better stories trail off, fearing perhaps the existential ramifications of doing what he used to do, digging and dancing in the minefields of our collective unconscious." That digging and dancing is expected of high art, even required, until, apparently, it is tainted with personal drama. When an artist's conduct is found to be indefensible, they are expected to self-flagellate instead. A power dynamic seesaws, and we are left wondering what it would be like if instead, the artist confronted the psychology of seduction and attempted an articulation.

Last year, I happened to watch Jean-Claude Brisseau's *The Exterminating Angels*, released just after the filmmaker was convicted of sexual harassment, in 2006. The charge concerned his manipulation of two women into performing sexual acts on camera by promising them roles in an erotic thriller (neither were cast). *The Exterminating Angels* meditates on this situation, opening with a scene in which a director, "Francois," is holding (and filming) auditions. When an actress doesn't get the part after masturbating in front of Francois and his camera, she publicly alleges abuse. The film traces a wavering line between sexual passion and the desire to be rewarded, or a desire for the power to reward. Francois tests his actresses' limits by filming them becoming aroused, while the fictional actresses admit to being aroused because they are being filmed. Taboos are broken. Motives are questioned. Things fall apart. Francois is a moving target for projections of both lust and derision. The film's panting horniness reads, at times, like an honest portrayal of the director's libido, and, at others, like yet another untenable powerplay. Francois is confused by his own willingness to let so much go to get the perfect, sexy shot, and the film's pornographic pacing leaves us bewildered as well. (Following his arrest, Brisseau insisted his films "use sexual feelings in the same way that Hitchcock used fears.")

The film received plenty of high praise. One critic (a man) wrote that though Brisseau's "dashing alter-ego in *Exterminating Angels* enjoys attention from a buffet of young, tantalizing women, I never got the queasy feeling that comes from, say, watching Woody Allen surround himself with willing lovelies. That's thanks to this director's unsparing curiosity in defining the dynamic between this established older man with a modicum of authority and these women, variously wracked by the tidal emotions of youth." Another (a woman) wrote, "It would be difficult to argue that there's anything remotely sordid about sex as scripter-helmer Brisseau films it. … There's a lot of deliberate humor to leaven the threat of pretentiousness, which is more than one can say for the average Catherine Breillat opus."

A few of Breillat's films unravel the sexualized power dynamics of a director and actors performing sex scenes as well, tacking on the taboo of an older woman wielding control on set. *Sex Is Comedy* is a decidedly unsexy movie about the making of a movie. The plot revolves around two nameless actor characters who can't stand one another. A director character, "Jeanne," wants to create romance where there is none, telling the actors to endure days of getting a sex scene right. Her insistence feels unwarranted, or stupid, until it becomes clear that *Sex Is Comedy* is based on the behind-the-scenes of Breillat's *Fat Girl*, released a year earlier, in 2001. For that movie, actor Roxane Mesquida performed several sex scenes with actor Libero De Rienzo. In *Sex Is Comedy*, Mesquida is back, playing an actress forced to be in sex scenes with an actor she despises.

Watching *Fat Girl* for the first time, I had assumed that Mesquida's uneasiness during scenes in which her character is slowly manipulated into losing her virginity was great acting. After watching a breakdown of the process, however, I can only see real unhappiness. Jeanne is ruthless, with almost no redeeming qualities. In this way, Breillat bares her own sadistic side with the steady eye contact of a true masochist, asking her audience to torture her with judgement. Instead of self-satirizing or seducing us into staying with her, she baldly recreates a problematic dynamic she once created, even hiring back the actress who suffered the original trauma this metanarrative depicts, ostensibly asserting the same power over her, all over again. *Sex Is Comedy* asks if *Fat Girl* was worth the trouble it took to make it. It offers no way out for those of us who love *Fat Girl*. We love it, after all, for its true-to-life depictions.

The first feature-length film C.K. directed, wrote, and starred in, *I Love You, Daddy*, was set to open in 2017. It was shelved after accusations of his sexual misconduct became public. The movie's publicity appeared to be further proof of C.K.'s cancelable character: from the black-and-white, jazz-inflected trailer, *I Love You, Daddy* looked like an homage to Woody Allen's late-'70s films. Even the title cards copied movies such as *Manhattan*, in which Allen's forty-two-year-old character dates a seventeen-year-old girl.

It's easy to find *I Love You, Daddy* as an illegal stream or torrent, even if it never got a wide release. Watching it now is disorienting, as the very texture of it seems to have anticipated C.K.'s call-outs. The choice of filmstock turns out to be a ruse, of sorts. The director character, "Leslie," who has a similar reputation to present-day Allen, is the film's antihero. A television producer, "Glen," played by C.K., is a fan of Leslie's films. He sees Manhattan through Leslie's eyes, as we must, via *Manhattan*-esque cinematography. Glen is aware of the rumors of Leslie's ephebophilia but chooses not to believe them. Regardless, he wants to work with him. When Glen's teenaged daughter gets involved with Leslie, though, a set of self-delusions is revealed. The internal negotiation isn't easy for us, either, as we are reminded of Allen's early films—the (for some, delightful) impact they have had on cinema and the self-serving pretensions we didn't notice at first, seeing as we were being seduced, too.

The cursed corner is too pat a metaphor, the old burned-out church, its spiritual insides licked away, its brick walls singed from the inside out: no man is a monument, no church is without its secrets. It is also a few blocks away from where I will one day happen to meet Louis C.K., where I will see a young man double back to take a video of him from outside the window of the restaurant where we sit. It's where people will hang on his every humble and wise and hilarious word, where a live musician will announce his presence on the microphone without asking his permission, and more strangers will try to capture his night out on their cameras, from every angle.

(Later, my friends and I debated the right way to have behaved. We all had a role to play in this scenario and had to be aware of this the whole time. I've always wanted a spread following *Us* magazine's "Stars—They're Just Like Us!" called "Stars—They're Not Like Us!," documenting the behavioral changes that come from being constantly scrutinized, and from knowing that one's everyday encounters are potentially life-changing events in each nonstar's life. Writing about meeting celebrities is stigmatized because it is also name-dropping, and so we've missed out on so many stories of what this feels like: being visited by someone from another world.)

I remembered my previous interactions with directors and actors and writers of whom I was a fan, men who had changed something for me through their work, and later, with their attention. I somehow always blew it, told them too much. Maybe they wanted to meet me, a devotee, and for it to be a certain way, but I could not figure out what way that was. They say never meet your idols, but they don't say why. The longer version of that is never meet your idols if you want to believe they are unbreakable. You are there to hold them up, not the other way around.

C.K.'s comeback tour received standing ovations but was torn apart by critics, again, for being sarcastically self-effacing instead of genuinely introspective. It could be that he doesn't have enough critical distance yet to look at his own situation clearly. It could also be, though, that he'll be forever in anguish over the backlash he and other artists have faced for exposing their exploitative desires in the industries built around exploitation. They're still under the radar, tenderly defensive, hiding in Europe, or talking about leaving everything behind, as if that's a possibility, instead of developing their own circumstances, asking, along with us, why this type of thing keeps happening, why entertainment will inevitably always articulate and generate power imbalances. Why I keep coming back to it.

Nowhere to Sit

The couch was unlike the image when it arrived. The roommates looked at it, delivered and out of the box, the first new piece of furniture they had bought as a group. It was supposed to be what brought the room together, something luxurious. They should have known that cheap velvet would look it, giving away more than what their secondhand or inherited furniture did.

"It looks shaved," said Jack.

"It's less blue than I thought," said Beatrice.

"It looks like a miniature that's been blown up," said Hugh.

They decided to return it, which meant losing the delivery fee and all that time.

"A good couch is expensive," said Hugh's mom on the phone.

He told himself to take a breath. "It was a good deal," he said. "It just wasn't exactly what we all wanted."

"You were trying to cut corners. That doesn't work out your whole life, you know."

When everyone was home, they decided to order Peruvian and eat it on the floor. It was a good deal when they bought a whole rotisserie chicken with four sides. "What if we spent more," started Hugh, and then he stopped.

"Because that's an option for everyone?" said Jack, for whom it was an option.

"I don't think the blue couch was that bad," said Selina, who was working when it was delivered and again when it was picked up.

She had missed the living room's air getting filled with its bluish fuzz and its hollow weight when it was lifted or set down.

"We could've put a blanket on it if it wasn't that soft."

"Then what's the point of getting it?" asked Jack.

"To have a couch." Selina gestured at the way they were sitting.

They all argued some old points, about what they wanted the couch to be. It had to be big enough for guests to sleep on, or it shouldn't be too big in case guests would assume they could sleep over. It had to be nice, so when their parents visited there was something different, something more adult about the place. It had to go with some other things. They had to get a coffee table next. Maybe they should have gotten that first. Maybe there was a way to get the whole apartment to match. What if they started with the place settings that were there when they moved in, which were that '90s style of abstract design framed in industrial white. Everyone hated them.

On the desktop computer they used mostly as a television, a show about weight loss streamed. No one was paying much attention to it until some dramatic music started. Someone had died during a routine surgery.

"I didn't know that happened."

"It happens all the time."

"No, that we see death on a show like this. It's morbid."

"It's realistic."

Theirs was a generation that wanted less because they were taught that excess was the worst. Minimal decoration, sans serif, hardy houseplants with no flowers. It was difficult enough that they all had to share this place, with their differing tastes and goals. Communal living was never really that unless everything was shared, and instead, there were three kinds of coffee in the freezer at all times, spilling out of their bags and leaving a dark dust on the ice trays. There was a joke about suspended adolescence sewn into every conversation: we should get a dog as a household, we should write a TV show about our lives, we should ask my newly divorced dad to move in with us. None of them would have chosen this life, they openly told one another, even though they all had, and could leave it at any time.

Before they even looked for another couch, they threw a party. The idea was that people could dance where there was no furniture. Since there was nowhere for anyone to sit, though, they stood against walls, sipping drinks like shy kids at school. Selina was working late again. They talked about how great she was, never complaining about the long hours she put in at the restaurant. Maybe she liked it there better than here, though, they wondered aloud. She didn't give any of them discounts anymore, come to think of it. It was her home away from home, away from all of them.

Guests filled the apartment, and the garbage can filled with trash. Hugh kept collecting disposable cups and bottles from the windowsills and floor, putting them into a big bluish bag that he'd then stuff into a closet.

"Stop cleaning, it's making people nervous," said Jack, but Hugh couldn't help it. He liked to stay busy around this many people. "And go get your friends out of the bathroom. They've been in there forever and now there's a line."

"Why are they all of a sudden *my* friends?" asked Hugh.

Selina came in the front door using her keys and saw Jack right away. Hugh rushed past her. Her eyes bulged in a knowing way. "I'm putting my stuff in my room," she mouthed, but Jack pushed through the crowd and caught up with her.

"Myla Gant is here."

"Myla Gant? Why?"

"No clue."

People were cheering inside the locked bathroom, as if watching a fireworks display.

"We're completely out of booze," said someone in the kitchen, peering into the fridge and then back at all of them with a look of panic.

Myla Gant was at Mark Cheever's house the next day. Mark Cheever, whom she had dated in high school. They had talked about marriage then—she did, at least, in front of their friends. When they were alone, or on the phone, though, neither of them brought up the future. To Mark, and to everyone, Myla was unserious. She had what his father described as a "wild streak." As they grew up and apart, Myla doubled down on both sides. Her wild streak became her whole self, and yet she'd still talk of settling down. With strangers in a public bathroom, almost asleep in the back of a cab, or over brunch in the West Village, she'd breathe, "I just want to be married."

She'd gone to the party in Brooklyn because Mark had told her about it, but once she was there, he'd decided not to go. The longer she stayed, the more out of place she felt. Myla was often the last person at a gathering, not because she fell into the moment, but because she couldn't find it. She was there longer because she'd felt the night had never truly started.

Mark didn't end up going out that night because he was exhausted from cleaning his parents' empty townhouse, getting it ready for his own party. It was Myla who had told him he should throw a party while they were gone. It was true what her friends had always said, that he didn't have much to offer, except that he wasn't a bad person, and he wasn't a bad-looking person, which, honestly, was a lot.

At Mark's, friends arrived in different stages of hunger, either going for the crudités, talking about the restaurant from which they'd just come, or, in one case, unwrapping a deli sandwich. Mark was worried that some of them were expecting more and wondered aloud if they should order pizza. "This isn't that kind of party, Mark," Grace corrected him. Grace was someone Mark had been seeing for about two months. Something in her voice had changed. She sounded drunk, or not drunk, but like an actor playing a drunk.

The doorbell kept ringing. Mark was happy to see Beatrice and Selina, two women he'd met while assisting his father on a photo shoot once. They were not from New York, probably, the kinds of people who took low-paying jobs as extras and production assistants in the hopes that these would lead to higher-paying jobs. Not *high*-paying jobs, just high*er*. People from outside the city didn't seem to think that far ahead. He apologized for having missed their soirée the night before. They looked at each other and shook their heads at him, insisting they weren't offended. Their eyes were wandering around the foyer. The townhouse spread out in all directions.

Mark led the new arrivals to the dining room, which was separated from the kitchen by an island lined with bottles, whole citrus fruits, and a martini shaker. Glass wall sconces held real candles. Someone described a framed advertisement for coffee in a foreign language as "probably racist." The guests never saw the other floors, but some, who had been to the house before, told the rest that there was a bowling alley and a sauna. New York townhouses are never as big as they aspire to be, even the ones decorated correctly, with vintage mirrors over marble half tables on every landing. They can only go up, and so each room is an anticipation of the next.

"Red or white?" asked Mark.

Selina pointed to a bottle the color of red and white combined.

Beatrice tried to start conversations with "What do you do?" and found that most of the people she met didn't work, per se, but some had started businesses or produced films. Many were not drinking, citing sober programs.

Someone screamed and continued to scream. Selina followed the crowd, thinking Beatrice was close behind her. Everyone was looking up through the center of a spiral staircase, at a boy standing on the banister. He was balancing, not threatening to jump, but stepping back and forth like a tightrope walker.

The girl screamed again. Now she was the one everyone was looking at. It was Grace, sitting in a doorway, holding her head.

"She's spiraling," someone said loudly, either used to it or unable to resist.

The boy hopped down. Grace was rocking back and forth, not any happier. The boy even skipped down the stairs and squatted in front of her to offer comfort, but she pushed his face away with a hand. Everyone was talking about life and death and madness.

"Come with me," said Myla. To Selina's surprise, the command was directed at her. Beatrice was gone, having left with a larger group, probably on her way to another party. Selina remembered watching Myla leave her own apartment the night before, beautiful and forlorn, probably drunk but poised. She'd looked so alone there, and here she was the opposite. People appeared drawn, physically, to her. When Myla spoke, or laughed with her whole body, moving whiplike through conversations, everyone in the house listened with at least one ear.

With soft, uncareful steps, Myla went up the stairs and Selina followed, as did Grace, now quiet and upright. They found themselves in a spotless, black-and-white tiled bathroom.

"Breathe," said Myla, lighting a cigarette. "You're fine." Grace sat on the bathmat and Selina perched on the tub. Myla opened drawers and read medicine labels, all uninteresting. She leafed through a lidded box of documents, hoping for a distraction, such as a revealing birth certificate or the house deed, but mostly found printouts from the time of reams with holes on each side, in strips that could be torn off. Each girl pictured herself tearing off those strips and throwing them away. It would be nice to have a job like that, a boring job. After work, all the people there would love to leave. They would feel truly free, as opposed to not, once every weekday, a perfect release, a "happy hour."

"So," Myla said to Selina. "What do you do?"

Later in the week, the roommates, Hugh and Beatrice and Jack and Selina, all miraculously had the day off, and so they took the J into Manhattan and from there, the Q down to Brighton Beach. It was crowded, but not as crowded as the other beaches nearby.

"So, Myla used to date Mark, forever ago," said Beatrice, describing the party at the townhouse. A man selling nutcrackers from a plastic cooler walked past them, calling out flavors. "Apparently, Grace is extremely jealous."

"That tracks," said Hugh.

"It's not true," said Selina.

The other three looked at her, over a distance growing between them. Four children ran toward the ocean, kicking up sand and screaming at the top of their lungs.

"Well, what's the story, then?" asked Hugh, finally.

"Oh, actually. I meant to tell you guys," said Selina. She was looking at the sky. "Mark wants us to have one of his sofas. His mother is redecorating."

The Girl

In some Patrick McMullen photos from 2004, an intimate party at Rick and Kathy Hilton's house is thrown to congratulate Donald Trump on his new series *The Apprentice*. Kathy and her daughter Paris are in head-to-toe Sanrio pink. A bedazzled phone hangs from Paris's pink beaded necklace. (Paris has multiple phones, which she has been seen carrying like a deck of cards. This way, she can conveniently lose one, or forget to take it with her somewhere, then come back to it later.) In one photo, she has added a tiara with pink gemstones to the pink flowers on her head. Her smile, like in most photos of her, is knowing and sad.

The women who wear all pink are aware of what they look like, I'm sure. Just like when you see the word *Pink* on a sweatshirt that isn't pink, you understand what it means. It means that girls just want to have fun, and part of having the fun that girls want is getting to cry and be left alone but looked after. I've always loved the color pink, so many women say to the camera, pretending they don't know that they're describing the color of a baby girl's room before she is even born—a gender, not a person, an expectation, not a reality.

In Vincent Gallo's 2001 "Honey Bunny" music video, women in their underwear sit and stand on a lazy Susan, being spun around. The only one who isn't holding still is Paris Hilton, who, on all fours, looks a little coked-out but beautiful, her short blonde hair in a loose ponytail. She is worlds away from the Paris of *Paris in Love*

(2021–22), a reality show about the original heiress influencer getting married to a Midwestern financier with no discernable taste. Paris gives him the nickname "Handsome" as if it's a joke and says to her friends: "A nice guy, finally."

"She's shy," Kathy keeps saying, in this show and in others. Apparently, that's why she puts on a baby voice or pretends to be on her phone. Paris herself says she's confronting past trauma and wraps up all her flaky behavior into one documentary storyline where she finally tells her family that she was abused at Provo Canyon School when she was a teenager.

"We only did this to save you," says Kathy, about sending her to Provo, after watching *This Is Paris* (2020) for the first time. "I mean, you were uncontrollable."

"I know," says Paris, without going into any more detail. Both mother and daughter wear mostly pink, still, and have every shade of pink in their homes. Earlier in the show, they argue over which types of pink are okay for the bridesmaid dresses and the wedding bouquets.

Vincent is in those Patrick McMullen photos of the *Apprentice* party, too. Even though this is after he wrote the song, "I Wrote This Song for the Girl Paris Hilton," his hand is holding Paris's sister Nicky's waist. Nicky, brunette at the time, wears a plain, lichen-colored dress. She is smiling or laughing, possibly because of something Vincent has whispered in her ear.

In the same way that Paris builds and rebuilds a fantasy of femininity, Vincent ensconces himself in breakable masculinity. He races motorcycles, plays guitar, knows the streets, films undressing women. He starts drama online, gets political, models in liquor campaigns (even though he doesn't drink and never has). He goes for the blonde, again and again (even if he gets along better with the brunette).

Around 2001, I cut out a photo from a tabloid magazine of Paris and Vincent in the backseat of a car and put it on my school binder because to me it was a perfect image. He's wearing what looks like a three-piece suit and she's wearing a hot pink tube top, a cigarette delicately suspended from her lips. He gazes at her with a look that is simultaneously fascinated, desperate, maybe even in love, but also pitying. On the pedestal in the "Honey Bunny" music video, Paris touches her hair, moves her hand slowly and nervously down her neck. Unlike the other girls, she does not look into the camera lens, or at anything.

"There was just no getting through to you," says Kathy, looking back at her decision to send Paris to that awful boarding school. Kathy would have never forgiven herself if she hadn't tried to curb Paris's teen misbehavior however possible, she explains, tearing up. Anyway, she adds, "You have to experience the darkness to appreciate the light."

Paris's aesthetic has grown increasingly tame, like a Valentine's Day store display. At forty-one, she's replaced her stringy extensions with a thick Barbie ponytail, her strappy sandals with pointed Valentino pumps. Everyone wants her to be the happy, carefree girl who sells the perfumes, or the energetic DJ who starts the party, she pouts. This is her excuse for hiding her past from her loved ones for so long. As a public explanation, it doesn't really track. Some of us, at least, instead romanticize the blasé runaway who was photographed with a different heir or actor every night, in the designer equivalent of thrashed Saint Marks T-shirts and mall kiosk rhinestones.

In my early twenties, the only famous person I had ever met was Vincent Gallo, after his band played a show in Detroit. I didn't live in Detroit, had never lived anywhere, I felt. Seeing his movies for the first time, back in high school, I was moved by a new concept:

What if the men who do terrible things—the guys with the motor-cycles and the guitars and the cameras—are the most sensitive, making up for some childhood pain? A year or two after I met him, Vincent was driving across the Southwest and called me from an unlisted number. I was alone in my apartment, doing nothing. "I want to go to your favorite restaurant," he said.

I got dressed and waited. "Anyone in this town you really hate?" he asked, once we'd had a Guatemalan dinner and met up with my friends. We were walking around, getting stares from people on the sleepy streets. I described a guy who cheated on his wife with teenagers and had been imprisoned for torture. Plus, I said, some-times this guy would come to my work just to laugh at me for having such a pathetic job and unimpressive life.

"Where is he?" Vincent asked.

I said I didn't know, since I didn't, but he ended up being at the very next place we went—the all-night diner—like everyone was, all the time.

"That's him?"

I was scared, suddenly. Maybe Vincent had come all the way to my hometown just to befriend my enemy, I thought. He could turn around and laugh at me, at us, at our whole stupid city. Maybe bad men are really bad, not sensitive, and *Buffalo '66* was a lie, told by one such man. That picture of Paris in the car with him—did she really have the upper hand? Did she hate his music video, like she hated her leaked sex tapes? What did he say to Nicky, to make her laugh? I can still remember this moment of fear. I still expect my world to turn inside out at any moment, especially the very best ones.

Instead, Vincent walked up to the bully and said that he was here to visit a very special, very fun person. He pointed at me. He didn't want to be friends with anyone who wouldn't want to be friends with me, he said. Nothing could have made me happier, even if it meant that the bully (who, it turned out, was a huge Vincent Gallo fan), would text me afterward to say that he knew where I lived.

I remember getting the occasional chatty phone call after that, never to make plans, just to help me through the endless days at work. Vincent talked about the women he had loved, the ones who had scared him. He liked my sister, who was blonde then, and we'd talk about that. He wanted every girl to be blonde, I could tell (I wasn't). I don't know when the phone calls stopped. I have a vague memory of walking around SoHo with Vincent after I moved to New York, and I could tell the novelty was fading. We had not enough and too much in common, then. I'd become a person, lived in a place.

"I feel good, I feel good, I blame you, I blame you," sings Paris Hilton in her song "I Blame You" (2020), which is excerpted during the *Paris in Love* intro. It's deceptively airy, begging an unserious listen as neon pink graphics flash and scroll. The sentiments behind "I feel good" and "I blame you" neutralize one another. Paris, the story goes, is recovering from a lifetime of damage by marrying a so-called nice guy, going to therapy, looking for a surrogate, leaving her clubbing days in the past. She's being honest for the first time, she says. And then, in an entirely pink-painted ice cream shop she's loved since she was a kid, she breaks down into tears, saying, "I just don't wanna be alone forever."

Hearing "I Blame You" is what reminded me of Vincent's song for Paris, which is also a study in adding depth to derived emptiness. His is jazzy and somber, but electric. "Honey Bunny" repeats pet names for girlfriends and the word *girlfriend* in a babyish voice, like it was written by someone who has never dated anyone, like the characters he plays in his movies. Be my girlfriend, says the man in a suit, to the woman in pink, who doesn't hear him or believe him or trust him, because she can't. There is something behind all those phones, that half-closed eye, that sad smile, the layers of blonde and diamanté, he thinks. There must be. For each, the moment is forever, and nothing is better than finding it, again and again. It feels good to get over things, but then they're over, and someone else is to blame.

Chelsea Hotel

"I feel starstruck just being here," says Patric, sitting on a tasseled purple couch with Bryn, Bobbi, and the *Buffalo* editors David, Adrian, Andrea, and Tati. We're in the eighth-floor two-bedroom suite where Madonna shot her book *Sex*, or at least we're pretty sure that's where we are, since the Hotel Chelsea's renovated rooms are now marked with letters instead of numerals. I arrive while a photo shoot is winding down and people are slowly leaving, not really wanting to. In anticipation of my stay here, I've been brushing up on the hotel's history by reading those articles that magazines like to publish every few years, the ones that collect quotes from all the famous people who used to live here and are still alive. The more I read, the more the place doesn't seem real, until I walk into it, and it is.

A psychic arrives, wearing a top hat and a silk scarf. He tells us that he's been in this suite before, back when he used to live at the Chelsea with his friend, the late Nicky Nichols. Tati is wearing a shirt with a picture of Sid Vicious on it that says "Drugs Kill" and swears it was not intentional, so we take it as a sign to ask about the famous murder that happened here. In fact, the psychic tells us that everyone who was here at the time of Nancy Spungen's death is sure that her boyfriend Sid didn't kill her. It was the drug dealer (drugs kill!). That's not telepathy though, he clarifies; it's common knowledge within these walls. He lights incense and fills a glass with water to absorb evil spirits, then consults his tarot deck. Sid is in another dimension, still distraught over that fatal, confused night, he tells us. Later that week, I meet a current tenant of the Chelsea who rolls her eyes when I tell her about our reading. "He said he used to live here? That's a new one."

Like anywhere with a famous history, the stories about what happened at the Chelsea aren't consistent. And this isn't some bar that boasts a visit from F. Scott Fitzgerald at the top of its menu, it's the legendary hotel where so many luminaries have stayed, referenced in so much media, that its name has become shorthand for another, better era—not a specific one, like when Edgar Lee Masters wrote "The Hotel Chelsea" (1936), when Leonard Cohen wrote "Chelsea Hotel #2" (1974), when Bob Dylan wrote "stayin' up for days in the Chelsea Hotel" ("Sara," 1976), when *Portrait of Jason* (1967) and *9½ Weeks* (1986) and *Léon* (1994) were filmed here, or when Charles R. Jackson, author of *The Lost Weekend* (1944), died in his room here (1968), one of a vast and unconfirmed number of suicides—but just some *other* era, when a scene was truly concentrated to one address, where tortured creative types could crash into each other every day, a hell and a paradise.

Everyone has some idea of what this hotel *was*, but most of the people I talk to about it don't seem to know what it *is*: a working hotel (again), with a new lobby bar and a fresh crop of tourists asking questions of the fresh crop of receptionists. While I'm staying in one of the luxe rooms on the seventh floor, tenants who have been here since the '90s pop their heads out of hand-painted doorways and walk their small dogs around the block as if nothing has changed as of late, which is understandable, since really, the building has been transforming dramatically since they moved in. The history of how many times this place has changed hands is long, storied, and full of controversy. It's uncomfortable, being here now and knowing that the renovations have caused tensions between and among the tenants, but then, that is the state of New York City, isn't it? It's the only New York I've ever known, at least: fun with an underbelly of disastrous gentrification. There is no party here that isn't in some way wrong for being what it is, sponsored or appropriating or excluding.

The Hotel Chelsea even appears anomalous in its war for lower rent because some of its tenants have succeeded in becoming cultural landmarks of their own, getting to stay in the pricey heart of Manhattan simply because they made the brave decision to locate here in the hotel's dilapidated days (the new Chelsea does not offer residential living). In the documentary that is in theaters at the time I'm staying here, *Dreaming Walls: Inside the Chelsea Hotel*, tenant Joe Corey says he would rather the renovations "never finish, because we couldn't afford it." The rent he shares with his wife Susan K after being moved from the rooftop to the first floor, he says, is about $317. "It will go up about $200 more," says Susan. One morning, I take a copy of the *Post* from the lobby and over a continental breakfast of berries and granola read "Average Manhattan rent breaks $5,000 for the first time in history."

That same morning, I leave for a meeting and come back to find that the scaffolding has been completely removed from the front of the building. Men are loading up the very last metal beams in a truck. Everyone walking by marvels at the red brick and ornate stained glass, naked for the first time in twelve years. I see some of the Chelsea's holdouts exit the lobby and look up, surprised by a lot more sunlight than usual on their doorstep. Everything is changing here all the time, and each change is contentious because it means someone might have to deal with a different class in their hallways, but I can't imagine that seeing the hotel's face again wasn't, if momentarily, a happy reunion for those who knew it before. (In *Dreaming Walls'* end credits, a little cross and the year 2020 is next to Joe's name; Susan now puts artist business cards in the lobby for guests who might be interested in buying her paintings).

Back in the *Sex* room, Tati is frustrated that a street-cast model has made off with a camisole and some underwear. It would be one thing if this person had been wearing them during the shoot, but since she wasn't, the theft feels too deliberate. Over the next few days, Tati talks with everyone involved to track down the missing fashion items, which are on loan from a brand and need to be returned. The model spends most of her time in Sheridan Square, we are told. Finally, a photographer comes straight from Greenwich Village into the suite with the missing items, triumphant and sweaty. His story: he'd been casing the park, asking around for her whereabouts or phone number, and instead of doxing her, the others started to talk. Word spread that she was stealing and lying about it, which was more embarrassment than she could bear, apparently, because she gave herself up. Her story: she thought they were complimentary.

Although the incident is an annoyance to the magazine, it is to be expected, seeing as the theme of this issue is the hotel that became famous for housing artists who couldn't live anywhere else in such style, or, hustlers. Historically, the guests with more money to spend and more to gain from hanging around the avant-garde indirectly subsidized the bills of the latter, handpicked by the late Stanley Bard. In all the old interviews about this place, people say the reason it was so great and weird was because of Stanley's fascination with the lives of artists and rich dilettantes alike, and his willful ignorance of the more destructive habits of each.

I go down to the Bard Room, named after the Bard family, which includes the "Robin Hood of innkeepers" (according to his

New York Times obituary, 2017), Stanley, who inherited his beloved managerial position from his father David, a stake owner of the hotel since 1947. The ceiling is original, I overhear someone say, and I look up to see a beautifully chipped and mottled molding. Much of this place was not preserved, instead restored to a level of luxury its current tenants don't remember. The 1884 Gothic Victorian was originally opened as Manhattan's tallest building and has gone through many turns that exemplify the New York experience, if exaggeratedly so: from residential co-op to luxury hotel and back again, and back again, like the ouroboros of big city neighborhoods getting regentrified every few years, but within one establishment. The stories of famous artists attracted other artists. In a popular clip of a young Patti Smith on the hotel's rooftop in the 1970s, she says she came to the Chelsea because of Dylan Thomas (he was checked in here when he died, in 1953). Now, a black-and-white photograph of Patti standing in front of the Hotel Chelsea sign with her then-roommate Robert Mapplethorpe is among the most iconic images of the place, on postcards and magnets and notebook covers.

In the Lobby Bar, I meet with a group of friends. Ebe grew up in New York and so of course has a Chelsea story. She saw her first porno movie here, in the apartment of a childhood friend, and she remembers the plot more than anything else: a man looking for his estranged daughters finds some women who want to have sex with him along the way, and he later discovers that these are the girls he was initially in search of. Daniel, who went to NYU, tells me he used to come here when Lola Schnabel had an apartment, a gift from her father Julian.

In his story "The Chelsea Affect," Arthur Miller says Mary McCarthy recommended it as a place to get away from the press, which is hard to imagine, seeing as he was here (according to the essay) when Andy Warhol was shooting *Chelsea Girls*, when Allen Ginsberg was hawking *Fuck You! A Magazine of the Arts* in the lobby, when Arthur C. Clarke was writing *2001: A Space Odyssey* here, and when Valerie Solanas would "show up in the lobby now and then," threatening to "shoot a man one of these days." In the story, the author speaks to the Bards about the problem with Valerie, "but they pooh-poohed the idea of her doing anything rash. As I slowly learned, they were simply not interested in bad news of any kind. Of course she shot Warhol two days later. ... It was not, one thought, that Stanley cultivated weird people, potheaded layabouts and some extraordinary as well as morbidly futile artistic types, but simply that he seemed to think these dreamers were normal; it was the regular people who made him uneasy."

So long as I'm in the area, I go to the new gallery Ulrik, on West Seventeenth, and meet with its curator, my friend Alex, who, when I tell him where I'm staying, says, "I peed in a hallway there once," and then clarifies, it was in a vessel, and it was a longer story. His friend's friend "Fanessa (with an *F*) lived there. I still have the hotel stationery where she wrote her number." Within each slot for the days of the week, Fanessa wrote, "Be fabulous." The artist Jim Fletcher arrives at the gallery. "The Chelsea?" he says, a faraway look in his eyes. I ask him if he has any stories about it and he answers, solemnly, "I do." The next thing he does is take out a plastic recorder and start playing it. I look at the group show that is up and try to make some connection between the artworks. The press release is not an explanation but a true story, told by the gallery's other curator's daughter, Fifi:

I have a 7th grade group chat, with my class and me. My class is made up of 15 people, a third of which I am friends with.

One of my friends, Tracy, has a picture that she doesn't like of herself. One other person in our group had this picture and sent it to the group chat without Tracy's consent. Tracy's first instinct was to say the picture wasn't of her, and instead to make up a friend named "Molly," who allegedly was the person in the photograph. I knew from the start who the picture was of, but I wanted to back up my peer because she was my close friend. Everyone agreed with Tracy, except for Emily who started saying things such as "she's lying" and "I swear that's a picture of her." We thought this was indecent of Emily, so we kept on defending Tracy. Soon enough Emily gave up. The subject was never brought up again.

I walk back to the hotel and up its famous stairwell, where multiple people have jumped (others went out the windows or overdosed in rooms) and workers are hanging up old art that was in storage for a long time: funny and not funny paintings and framed photographs made by previous tenants who probably paid Stanley this way. One, a colored pencil drawing under glass, depicts Sid and Nancy in their room. Later, in the Lobby Bar, I meet a family who have lived here since the '90s: author/lawyer Michael Rips, his wife, artist/former model Sheila Berger, their daughter Nicolaia Rips, who at seventeen wrote a memoir about growing up here and was named "the Eloise of the Chelsea Hotel" by *W* (2016), and a large black poodle-like dog that gently puts his head and front paws in my lap.

In Abel Ferrara's 2008 documentary *Chelsea on the Rocks*, Michael wears a suit and pocket square while Sheila, barefoot and in jeans, sits on a leather chair in their apartment. "This figure," he says, pointing to a sculpture on their shelf, "is an African fetish from the Bamana tribe. It is entirely constructed of human feces, over the top of which women menstruate in order to feed the object. Stuffed inside are the bones of small children in the tribe who have passed away, and they insert the bones through the anus of the fetish figure." The clip is sandwiched between other tenants talking about their September 11 experiences. I can hear Ferrara muttering "Jesus" while Michael describes his art collection, the lawyer's dry humor, which I've now seen firsthand, apparently lost on the director.

Later in the documentary, the actress Gaby Hoffmann, who, like Nicolaia, grew up here, goes against the grain by saying something not completely fawning about Stanley. Her relationship with him, she says, "was miserable because when I was six and walking through the lobby on my way to first grade, he would pull me into that creepy, dark, dusty little office of his and tell me that if I didn't get my mother [the Warhol superstar Viva] under control, that we were gonna be evicted."

In fact, a few people have mentioned Viva as the person with perhaps the most contentious relationship with her neighbors and landlords at the Chelsea, which sounds like a real feat. Gaby, for her part, has a complicated view of the place because of that and maybe also because it represents a complicated concern: How much should we treasure the memories and fantasies of a time that valued artists more for their eccentricities? As Viva herself recalled ("Where the Walls Still Talk," *Vanity Fair*, 2013), "One night, a guy from a floor above us landed on a metal table in the courtyard—on his head. The very next day another guy jumped out the window onto the synagogue next door. ... He was being carried down the hall on a stretcher. I asked him, 'Why did you jump out the window?' He said, 'Because John Lennon was shot.'" By the time R. Crumb was here, in the early 2000s, he said, the other guests "were all arty-farty pretentious people with money who wanted to stay there because Sid and Nancy lived there. That was my impression, anyway. The whole thing seemed extremely self-conscious to me."

In an introduction to *Hotel Chelsea: Living in the Last Bohemian Haven*, Gaby writes to her sister Alex Auder: "if I'm gonna write anything do I wanna write the foreword to someone else's book about how bohemian the bohemians are and how cool it is that I was raised by an artist bohemian enough to live there in the mecca of bohemianism and what a loss and oh the city and all those hideous chase banks and what about that old bum on the stoop I would chat with every day while eating my soggy éclair from the corner donut shop that is now a starbucks." By the end of the exchange, though, the two have become nostalgic for the way of life that made them who they are, each herself a mother now. Doing "nothing," says Alex, is "what mom got famous for and what Warhol captured in his movies. ... Now even nothing is being commodified." "Yes," Gaby replies, "mom raised us right."

The photographer Tina Tyrell is waiting for Narcissister and Miranda July to get out of hair and makeup so she can photograph them on the piano in the Lobby Bar. We know each other, she says, and remembers a luncheon where we were both guests, at the Four Seasons, another Manhattan landmark that has morphed a few times. "I stayed here for a couple of days when I first moved to New York," Tina tells me, "because I'd never heard of another hotel here." Tina is from LA and as a teenager made friends with Rufus Wainwright, son of Loudon Wainwright III and Kate McGarrigle, and Lorca Cohen, daughter of Leonard Cohen and Suzanne Elrod. "I decided to move to New York for Lorca's birthday on September 1, 2000, and I met Zaldy then, because Rufus became friends with all these Club Kids from the '90s that were like a tight group of friends from that Limelight period with Michael Alig and that whole drama, *Disco Bloodbath*. It was a whole scene. It was before my time, but it was still in the air."

Anyway, she never lived here, but she did come to the Chelsea for Zaldy's parties and also a dentist. "He was in 614 or something, and that had been Arthur Miller's apartment." Where was his office? I ask. "His office was here, in the building." Their relationship became fraught, she remembers, when he insisted that she get her braces taken off for a cleaning. She never got them replaced, and still wears Invisalign. I'm looking at her teeth, and she has an adorable gap between the front two. "Don't correct that," I say. "That gap I actually got from the dentist here—I just thought of that." Maybe he's an artist, I suggest. "He is! He made his own wine."

Nostalgia is a poison but forgetting is just as toxic. I compare the utopian stories about this place to what art is being talked about in New York now. This summer, at a gallery opening's after-party on the terrace of a building in which only billionaires live, a man strikes up a conversation with me. Not an hour later, he asks if I'm the same person he'd been talking to earlier. I sense he isn't drunk, just unsocialized. "Is that Anna from Twitter?" he blurts. "I've gotta get a picture." He wants Anna to hold up a phone, I think, in the hopes that he gets an image of someone with viral tendencies to inadvertently endorse an NFT, raising its value. He seems uninterested in art, and apparently uninterested in what Anna does, admitting upon meeting her that he's never listened to her popular podcast. Others at the party include supermodels and Leonardo DiCaprio. It feels very 2012, more than one person says to me, despite it being the first-ever NFT Week.

That same week, I find myself in SoHo, at a party that feels like another type of throwback as well as a simulation: avatars dance on screens while specialty cocktails are handed out, sushi chefs make handrolls in the middle of a dance floor, and girls get actual tattoos. I'm talking to the event's publicist when she says she has to shift gears because she's also a DJ and about to go on. The party favors are ginger shots and CBD chocolate. I recognize no one and can't understand what's being celebrated, exactly. When I leave, there's still an anxious crowd waiting to get in.

On the other hand, when I go to the opening of O'Flaherty's open-call art show, which has completely mobbed multiple blocks in Alphabet City and is being shut down by cops, nothing feels ironic. The art ranges from amateur to acclaimed and is crammed together, kind of like what's hung in the Chelsea's hallways. The crowd is young, having an impromptu block party in the evening heat, drinking beers from cans and ducking through open hydrant sprays. They filter into the nearby bars and talk excitedly about the show they couldn't even glimpse.

Weeks later, at Lucien, I'm at a table with O'Flaherty's founder Jamian, as well as a few prominent art dealers and some pretty girls. "No shade but you're ruining art," the gallerist yells, her raspy voice blending in with the din of wine glasses kissing and steak knives sawing. She is doing tequila shots instead of her usual whiskey straight from the bottle, but she doesn't seem the drunkest one here by far. All the art dealers agree that Jamian's selling herself short by opting to sell her own paintings through a niche New York gallery, its only value the sort of reverberating relevance of its founders. One of them says, "Mike Kelley died with a broken heart."

"And broke," Jamian adds, and then, "but that's all you care about, is money, and NFTs." She's in top form, fingers pointing wildly, listing the reasons behind each of her artworld decisions, including opening a gallery where every featured artist is allowed to do whatever they want, with the gallerists' full support, no matter how unsellable it is. Everyone at the table is unfazed, used to her and to these conversations. "Oh!" a new arrival says to Jamian, "I follow you on Instagram!"

I'm not in Chelsea often and it's fun to be a tourist on Twenty-Third Street, noticing what others before me have described as New York's quintessential characters: a bodybuilder with short blonde dreadlocks walking with a taller female friend and a dazed expression, a man trying to stab me with a cigarette butt he has just picked up off the sidewalk, families and teenagers and old people stopping to take photos of the hotel's façade. Men in trucks move velvet furniture into the dining areas while a fashionably dressed duo removes dead bushes from concrete planters to replace them with live bushes of the same species. A photo shoot is happening on a balcony visible from the street. A coiffed, blonde, statuesque model in a floor-length gown poses in front of the neon sign just as Dee Dee Ramone or Patti and Viva once did. It really does feel like we're in another time, not any particular one, but just not whatever is being called *now*.

Inside the Chelsea's restaurant El Quijote, a still-life shoot is underway. As fog from a machine obscures a portrait of Robert Mapplethorpe, the photographer jokes, "Robert who?" because we actually are living in the now, if fogged by this place's past, which, because it is the past, is telling us we can't measure up. A doorman mentions the *energy*: Can you feel it? I can feel a respect for the conventions of the unconventional. The sense of humor needed to serve drinks to a bar of European sightseers, old New Yorkers, punk transplants, high rollers, historians, and us.

Leaving the hotel is hard. One gets used to luxury quickly, it turns out, and I'm jealous of the people who can write whole books about living here, about all the things they've seen offhand that the rest of the world cares so deeply for and seeks out. And at the same time, I feel a burden of memoir lifting as I walk all the way across the island and downtown, thinking of a quote I recently read from Gerard Malanga: "I have no sentimental attachment, none whatsoever to the Chelsea. I think the best thing that can be done with it—and I say this with the hope that its architectural integrity be preserved—is that some hotelier take it over and transform it into the luxury hotel it's begging to be."

Fashion Week

A friend takes me to a pair of launches: an in-store in Chatham Square and a party in Ridgewood. Everything is really just a party in the end, made to give customers and press an idea of what the brand is: fun, maybe young, maybe rich. If, as another friend tells me, the biggest event on this fashion week's schedule is the anniversary of a bag, we're at the point of admitting what's really going on here.

From what I've seen so far, I can tell you: sliders are still in, roughed up with some jalapeño relish, as are mini tostadas, adorable falafel balls on lettuce tongues, and chicken salad on slivers of watermelon from near the rind. And I can say that increasingly, I see complex, premixed mocktails alongside full bars that offer no interesting cocktails. At Avant Gardner (a giant, ugly venue surrounded by waste management services, recycling centers, a garbage truck garage, and retail suppliers on all sides—trash, trash, trash, and trash), we wander around two giant inflated people in sexy poses. I end up at a friend's party in my neighborhood, too wasted to have a conversation.

The next day, I'm at a pop-up that has me sign a waiver, enter my information, and get okayed by the head of PR there before I'm allowed inside. It's called Some Warehouse Thing at NYFW, even though it is at a coffee shop, in the daytime, and not affiliated with a fashion line. It is, as far as I can tell, the launch of a digital skin collection designed in collaboration with a YouTube tutorialist. Photographers are everywhere, documenting the small crowd as we touch iPads connected to bigger screens to swap out features on avatars that live in the metaverse, get drinks in branded rubbery cups, pick up swag—matchbooks, stickers, Tamagotchis—and sit down at a craft table to bedazzle or stud or marabou-line an old band T-shirt from a rack. A friend shows me a meme, a "party girl checklist" that starts with the question "Are you actually having fun here?" and ends with the advice "These gays don't control your life." Even with that in mind, I end up at another pop-up, an expensive dinner, and another Ridgewood party.

This week, it was reported that an Arctic mass previously thought to be the northernmost piece of land in the world was actually a "dirty iceberg" all along. Never having seen an iceberg, when I see the word *iceberg*, the popular metaphor is more easily conjured than the real object: a grossly misleading surface standing for something it is not—something incalculably large and cold. I notice darkness pitching around, an ambiguous threat hanging in the air. Models, with their icy gazes and horsey trots, appear more ruthless, more determined. As the playing field spreads open and the runway attempts accurate representation, castings become anyone's game.

At shows and after-parties and dinners, friends tell me about the way someone is acting not like their self, someone is dressed desperately, some people are still not speaking, someone is much more depressed about the situation than they're letting on, a few of us have unhealthy relationships with drugs, a few more than we want to admit. In front of my apartment, I see the ugliest rat I've ever seen, and that's saying a lot.

Writing about what goes on in one person's schedule over the course of five days invariably exposes such a set of themed events as tip-sized in comparison to New York's dirty iceberg. Like, the

Armory Show is going on, too, as are the million theater openings and academic lectures and town halls and whatever else is always happening here, plus, you know, the Emmys, the Venice Film Festival, and everything everywhere else.

I go to a fashion show and the afterparty, which is an early afternoon cocktail, and once again I am stuck in an undercurrent of socializing that later contributes to some bad decisions. Since there are hours to kill before a dinner reservation, a friend and I buy a bottle of wine and drink most of it while pretending to recharge. The outfits we change into are sheer, his depicting a nude woman being groped by Satan, mine painted with skulls and the word *fetish*.

Now that I've decided to not smoke, I'm aware that one still needs to go out "for air" every once in a while, which is, I guess, what the rooftop at the Boom Boom Room is good for, but it is somehow even stuffy up there. This penthouse, with its mazed hallway of bathrooms, its fur-lined bathroom with one four-person toilet, and a conjoined club, Le Bain, were designed to house secrets, to hide tears, and to let people quietly leave, alone if they'd like. My friend and I wait outside for others to find us while a woman in a white outfit sits down on the sidewalk and leans all the way back. The man she is with pulls at her arms as she makes herself limp, closes her eyes. "No, stop it right now," he shouts, not for the first time. Without acknowledging this, since there is no reason to, we agree that our other friends can catch up with us on their own and hail a cab. On the way to the next party, I decide to skip it. In my staccato dreams, chunks of my skin are rotting, like that half-naked rat with a tumor growing out of its chopped-off tail I saw the previous night.

On my way to a show, I walk past the Bowery Whole Foods and notice someone's spilled groceries—a broken jar of kimchi and a fully intact kiwi. I say aloud, "A kiwi and a kimchi." The alliteration nauseates me, like a coding error, "a glitch in the matrix." Leaving another show, I notice a painting in the window of Half Gallery on East Fourth Street, of a woman with her face in the crook of one arm, the picture of despair. Not one block west, on the door of the Connelly Theater, a photo of Kate Berlant shows the comedian in the exact same position, distraught but sarcastically so. Furthermore, Kate herself is walking in front of me, on her way to the theater. "This is a glitch," I start to say, but I'm with a different set of people, and so it doesn't make sense to go into it.

I go to two different fashion shows that start an hour and fifteen minutes late. I go to something at the Times Square Hard Rock Hotel, hosted by a company for which I briefly worked, out of morbid curiosity. The event is, according to the invite, "a night where fashion and music come together [to] showcase artists, designers, dancers, and young creatives in a series of performances as well as a fashion show ... focused on sustainability, diversity, and equality in fashion ... to give voice to all creators, and raise awareness ... also celebrate our home, New York City." I haven't heard of this company doing anything in years and had assumed they'd closed shop, but, according to the founder once she takes the stage, they have become a nonprofit, shifting course during the pandemic to focus on what's important: raising awareness for the foundation, which, from what I can tell, is the company itself, rebranded as a nonprofit. She asks for less-harsh lighting, and for guests to get off the dance floor so that a special performance can take place. First, though, a moment of silence for September 11. And next, a video: something to explain what we are all doing here—except it plays at double speed; teenagers from different New York neighborhoods speak in comically high-pitched voices. Then, the video goes to half speed, and all these teens' voices become too low to understand. It goes back to too-fast again. Then it is over. I wonder how much it had cost to make. Next, a band takes its place behind microphones and a drum set and starts in on a song I don't immediately like, at all. The lead singer looks out of place here, although, to be fair, most people would. A man in a tight denim outfit is behind them, doing an interpretive dance.

I ask for water from the bar and am handed a big bottle of Billionaires Row Water. I read its fine print: "Billionaires Row's brand mission is to inspire and empower individuals to reach for their dreams, while protecting human welfare and advancement by furthering private initiatives for the good of the public by focusing on love for humanity, quality of life and planet preservation." My friend and I can't take any more and go to the Times Square Taco Bell Cantina, which is a wild place, too. Outside, a woman in a white skirt with a ten-foot radius twists in place. A photographer takes pictures of her while an assistant adjusts the outfit, trying to ignore a man getting closer to them, screaming about the world being on its way out, and the rain.

Another show is held on a helipad near the Staten Island Ferry. The view is impossible to dislike: skyscrapers behind the highway on one side, black water and the edge of Brooklyn on another, a drone hovering overhead, the moon massive and yellow, the Statue of Liberty finding her light. The models are like circus ponies before the patina-green barker on her pedestal, the bridges like red-and-white-dotted trapezes, the rest expanses of shadow beyond the follow spot.

Wrong Turn

I was in an Uber Pool (I guess it's not called that anymore) with some stranger, each of us going to Brooklyn from Manhattan. Our driver crossed the Williamsburg Bridge, took the first exit, then followed its loop all the way back onto the bridge, going in the opposite direction, reentering Manhattan. I wasn't paying attention. My co-rider looked up, at the skyline that was supposed to be behind us, and said something. "Are we going the wrong way?" Our driver laughed. Yes, he had made a wrong turn.

This was a very time-consuming "wrong turn." We had to go all the way back over the bridge, then get off somewhere in the Lower East Side and find a way back onto Delancey, which isn't simple, since U-turns aren't possible, there are so many one-way streets, and there's always traffic. My co-rider wasn't done asking our driver questions. What was he doing, instead of watching for the exit? He laughed again and pointed to a phone that was mounted to the left-hand side of his windshield, away from the GPS, which was mid-dash.

"What is that, a gossip website?" she asked. I looked at the small screen (phones were smaller then), making out a pink-and-purple layout, tiny photos of celebrities, text moving upward, ticker-like, in another language, maybe Korean, hearts and sparkles and whatever animating everything. It would be impossible to make out one headline, much less read these articles, and drive, I thought, and I guess that was being proven. Our driver was still smiling, pointing as if we could see the miniaturized information, as if we could read the foreign text and recognize the faces.

I knew from his wordless gestures that something huge had just happened to one of these celebrities, and he was too excited by this event to care about anything else. I was not as mad about the tardiness the detour had caused as I was about the ambivalence toward it, the way this guy was so elated by some gossip—or more likely the way in which he received such gossip, in the middle of one of those maneuvers that make his job obnoxious, like taking the first exit off a bridge—that he could forget about it, about us.

It was a moment that resonated with me more than it had to because it felt like the beginning of some next phase. Already, I was disappointed by a lot. When I was in college, professors would talk about "cocktail parties," as in "something overheard at" one, and I imagined that once I was done with my academic duties, I could apply all the theories and metaphors I'd learned to conversations, creating a context of higher education that would carry me through networks and nightlife and dependent relationships.

But then I was at cocktail parties, and there was never not some play-acting aspect to them. Here we are, at a thing that was meant for people who had more to offer, when people could offer more. We're only worth what we can promise later, now, I am told, in so many ways. It's all potential, anticipating some later engagement. The real action happens on the highway, in cars heading home to outer boroughs, a recap of everything that was missed while we were being handed champagne flutes—and come on, champagne flutes? It's all a joke, isn't it, that we're even here?

In my therapist's office, I try to stay on topic, but of course it comes down to this, to the crossroads of writer's block. I'm not even a writer, I whine, I just went to school for it for six years, tutored, taught classes, took writing jobs, edited others, published, and then, *you know.*

Is it something you're feeling about yourself, or about the world? she asks, I think, although I'm not really listening. I'm looking at the Dunkin' cup I'm holding, which is marked with red-and-green lettering for Christmas. The exact hues—holly berry and evergreen needle—represent two of the only plants that keep their color in winter, in a certain part of the world (this part). I point to the cup. "This was a choice," I say to my therapist, who knows I am hijacking, making the session into a presentation, so I stop myself. I never even say the word "Christmas" anymore, by force of habit, but those colors aren't meant for some other holiday.

Everything can't be so weighted, or else the words all sit too heavily on the page, each sentence a sign, a headline, a quote. "You can't use quotation marks when your subject is thinking," an old boyfriend once said to me. "That just looks like an echo." Because the way letters look *does* affect the way we read them, obviously, and that goes beyond typefaces, colors, the religions those typefaces and colors reference, the contexts in which the words are read. We can think punctuation, like a double set of quotation marks, is simply too like the comic strip code for *quivering* or *resonating*: short, concentric, semicircular dashes on each side of someone or something. (Thought, in a comic strip, is in a cartoon cloud, and it is connected to its thinker by a dotted line instead of a speech bubble's pointed tail.)

What do greeting cards say inside them, now? They still exist, at least in the Duane Reade across the street, but I never open them up. In another era, it was always a joke about aging, about needing a stud, about getting uncontrollably drunk because it's your day to, about how this card is all you're getting, not a prostitute as pretty as the one pictured on it. Now, maybe they are all blank, although I doubt that, because writing is everywhere, all the time, filling up the bubbles that are tethered to our brains.

I'm addicted to reading gossip, too, especially when it gets close to my life, threatening to destroy us. I pictured that Uber driver steering me, this stranger, and himself right into oncoming traffic and never breaking his smile, already having escaped into this little world I couldn't translate. He could have been reading a set of codes simply for the pleasure of decoding. Sparkle, heart: newness, love, nothing more than that, like the words *season's greetings* or a cold red and a colder green on the outside of a steaming coffee cup. "Sometimes," reads the inside of a card about friendship or something, "it's all you need."

Earlier versions of these stories were first published in the following places:

"Is Anyone Listening to Me? I Love It." In *Logue*, blue issue, ed. David Fishkind (2015); and in *Excellences & Perfections*, ed. Amalia Ulman (Prestel, 2018).

"My Best Friend in High School." In *Sex*, no. 10, ed. Asher Penn (2015).

"The Dollhouse." In *Affidavit* (online), ed. Hunter Braithwaite, June 18, 2019.

"Difficult." In *L'Officiel Hommes USA*, ed. Joseph Akel, Spring 2019.

"Rock, Paper, Scissors." In conjunction with Anna Uddenberg's *Privé*, at Marciano Art Foundation, Los Angeles, July 25–December 1, 2019.

"Pleasure." In *A Woman's Right to Pleasure*, ed. Alexandra Weiss (BlackBook, 2020).

"The Planet." In *El Planeta Film Companion*, ed. Amalia Ulman (Arcadia Missa, 2020).

"The Wheel." In *CR Men*, no. 9, ed. Patrik Sandberg (Fall–Winter 2019).

"The Cave." In *Artforum* (online), ed. Zack Hatfield, January 20, 2020.

"Apocalypse." In *Spike Art Magazine*, no. 63, ed. Rita Vitorelli, Spring 2020.

"New York, 2020." In *SSENSE* (online) ed. Olivia Whittick, April 14, 2020.

"Subculture." In *Frieze*, no. 218, ed. Andrew Durbin, April 2021.

"The World." Part in *Frieze* (online), ed. Andrew Durbin, October 12, 2020; and part in *Aperture*, no. 242, ed. Michael Famighetti, Spring 2021.

"Transplant." In conjunction with Alexander Carver's *Potent Stem*, at Kraupa-Tuskany Zeidler, Berlin, June 19–August 2021.

"Conspiracy." In *Gagosian Quarterly*, ed. Wyatt Allgeier, Spring 2022.

"The Director." In *Spike Art Magazine* (online), ed. Adina Glickstein, August 2, 2021.

"Nowhere to Sit." Part in conjunction with the group show *Dreamhouses* (online, at fortmakers.com), 2022; and part in conjunction with Rosetta Getty's Resort 2022 collection.

"The Girl." In *Buffalo Zine*, no. 15, ed. Andrea Lazarov (Spring–Summer 2022).

"Chelsea Hotel." In *Buffalo Zine*, no. 16, ed. Andrea Lazarov (Autumn–Winter 2022–23).

Natasha Stagg is the author of a novel, *Surveys*, and a collection, *Sleeveless: Fashion, Image, Media, New York 2011–2019*.